Kenneth Deighton

The Old Dramatists

Conjectural readings on the texts of Marston, Beaumont and Fletcher, Peele,

Marlowe, Chapman, Heywood, Greene, Middleton, Dekker, Webster

Kenneth Deighton

The Old Dramatists
Conjectural readings on the texts of Marston, Beaumont and Fletcher, Peele, Marlowe, Chapman, Heywood, Greene, Middleton, Dekker, Webster

ISBN/EAN: 9783337303921

Printed in Europe, USA, Canada, Australia, Japan

Cover: Foto ©Thomas Meinert / pixelio.de

More available books at **www.hansebooks.com**

THE OLD DRAMATISTS
CONJECTURAL READINGS

ON THE TEXTS OF

MARSTON: BEAUMONT AND
FLETCHER: PEELE: MARLOWE
CHAPMAN: HEYWOOD: GREENE
MIDDLETON: DEKKER: WEBSTER

BY K. DEIGHTON

Westminster
ARCHIBALD CONSTABLE AND CO.
1896

PREFATORY NOTE

MOST of the conjectures in this volume upon the texts of Marston, Beaumont and Fletcher, Peele, and Marlowe, with some that I have withdrawn, were printed for private circulation in 1894. These were so kindly received by several eminent scholars that, having now added six more of the old dramatists to my list, I venture to ask for a wider hearing.

Something in the way of apology should perhaps be said of an attempt which covers so large a field, especially as most of the dramatists with whose texts I deal have been subject to the criticism of many able editors and to the exercise of much sagacity. That I should hope to succeed where great names have failed may seem presumptuous. I am not, however, unmindful of the dangers of conjectural criticism, nor of the warnings addressed to would-be emendators. Among such warnings none perhaps is more to the point than that of the late Dr. Ingleby when he says in his *Shakespeare Hermeneutics*, p. 114: 'The simple truth is, that successful emendation is the fruit of severe study and research on the one hand, and of rare sensibility and sense on the other. The number of really satisfactory conjectures are comparatively few; and few are those critics who have shown any remarkable sagacity in this kind of speculation.'

Now I, of course, make no claim whatever to 'rare sensibility and sense'; I cannot dignify my reading as 'severe study and research'; still less do I imagine myself endowed with those excellent gifts so justly ascribed to scholars and critics like Theobald, Steevens, Dyce, and others of the past. At the same time, I shall be disappointed if these conjectures of mine are not recognised as the outcome of much patient industry, and of considerable familiarity with the language and thought of our old dramatists.   K. D.

THE OLD DRAMATISTS: CONJECTURAL READINGS

I. MARSTON[1]

1. *Antonio and Mellida*, i. 1. 258 :—

'*Ros.* Sweet Lady, nay good sweet, now by my troth
We'll be bedfellows: *dirt on compliment froth!*
  Exeunt; ROSALINE *giving* ANTONIO *the way.*'

Bullen explains the last words of the speech thus: 'No empty compliments! take the lead.'

In spite of the closer similarity of spelling between *troth* and *froth*, I would read, 'dirt on compliment! *forth!*'

1. *Antonio and Mellida*, ii. 1. 14 :—

'*Dil.* Upon mine honour.

'*Cat.* Your honour with a paugh! 'slid, now every jackanapes loads his back with the golden coat of honour; every ass puts on the lion's skin and roars his honour. Upon your honour? By my lady's pantable, I fear I shall live to hear a vintner's boy cry "'Tis rich neat canary." Upon my honour!'

---

[1] The references are to Bullen's edition, 2 vols., 1887.

The inverted commas should come after *honour!* not after *canary*; the words "'Tis rich ... honour!' being part of the boy's cry.

1. *Antonio and Mellida*, iii. 2. 9 :—

> 'I have walk'd all night,
> To see if the nocturnal court delights
> Could force me envy their felicity:
> And by plain troth, I will confess plain troth,
> I envy nothing but the *travense* light.
> O, had it eyes, and ears, and tongues, it might
> See sport, hear speech of most strange surquedries.
> O, if that candle-light were made a poet,
> He would prove a rare firking satirist,
> And draw the core forth of imposthum'd sin.'

For *travense* Bullen conjectures *traverse*, '*i.e.* light cast slantwise.' I can see no point in such an explanation, but would read *tavern's*.

1. *Antonio and Mellida*, iii. 2. 107 :—

For *dramatis persona Dil.* read *Cat.* Dildo has not entered yet.

1. *Antonio and Mellida*, iii. 2. 125 :—

'By the sugar-candy sky, hold up the glass higher, that I may see to swear in fashion. O, one *loof* more would ha' made them shine; God's neaks, they would have shone like my mistress' brow.'

Bullen says 'there is no meaning in the word "loof,"' and proposes 'touch': may not *loof* mean *turn, i.e.* of the barber's hand?

1. *Antonio and Mellida*, iv. 1. 70:—

> 'O you that *made open* the glibbery ice
> Of vulgar favour view Andrugio.'

For *made open*, Bullen gives *slide upon*, and *upon* is evidently right. But the change of *made* should, I think, be to *make*. In the sense of 'move,' *make* is frequent in the dramatists with prepositions and conjunctions, *e.g.*, to make to, towards, after, away forth, from, up, etc.

1. *Antonio and Mellida*, iv. 1. 80:—

> 'O rotten props of the crazed multitude,
> How still you double, falter under the lightest chance
> That strains your veins! Alas, one battle lost,
> Your whorish love, your drunken healths, your houts
>   and shouts,
> Your smooth God save's, and all your *devils last*,
> That tempts our quiet to your hall of throngs.'

In l. 80, for *devils last*, I propose *devils' lust*. Bullen gives *devils lost*, which makes scarcely better sense than *devils last*, to say nothing of *lost* being used two lines above. After *throngs* something has apparently dropped out, to the effect of 'are heard no more,' or an aposiopesis should be marked.

In l. 77, I fancy that *double* and *falter* were originally alternatives, one of which, probably *falter*, Marston forgot to erase.

II. *Antonio and Mellida*, i. 1. 73 :—
> 'That fair show
> Of *death*, for the excessive joy of his fate
> Might choke the murder.'

For *death*, I would read *grief*.

II. *Antonio and Mellida*, i. 1. 76 :—

'Whose *sinking* thought frightened my conscious heart.'

For *sinking*, perhaps *soaking*. Compare *The Winter's Tale*, i. 2. 224,

> 'Was this taken
> By any understanding pate but mine?
> For thy *conceit is soaking*, will draw in
> More than the common blocks.'

Piero, as Bullen remarks, dreads lest his villainies should be detected by Feliche.

II. *Antonio and Mellida*, i. 2. 130-132 :—

Balurdo, 'a rich gull,' is relating a dream he has had.

'For methought I dreamt I was asleep, and methought the ground yawned and belkt up the abhominable ghost of a misshapen simile, with two pages; the one called master, even as going before; and the other mounser, even so following after; whilst Signor Simile stalk'd most prodigiously in the midst.'

On this Bullen remarks, 'Balurdo is talking arrant nonsense.' But punctuate as follows, and it will be seen that Balurdo is (for him) talking excellent sense: The one called master 'even as,' going before; and the other, mounser (*i.e.* monsieur) 'even so,' following after; whilst, etc.

II. *Antonio and Mellida*, ii. 1. 58:—
 'He that's ambitious-minded, and but man,
 Must have his followers beasts, *damn'd* slavish sots,
 Whose service is obedience, and whose wit
 Reacheth no further than to admire their lord,
 And stare in adoration of his worth.'

The old editions give *dub'd*: read *dumb'd*. Cf. *A.C.* i. 5. 50,
 'what I would have spoke
 Was beastly *dumb'd* by him;'
Theobald's certain conjecture for *dumbe* of the earlier folios.

II. *Antonio and Mellida*, ii. 1. 154:—
 'The port-holes
 Of sheathèd spirit are ne'er *corb'd* up,
 But still stand open, ready to discharge
 Their precious shot into the shrouds of heaven.'

Bullen, who prints *corbèd*, remarks, 'Corbèd (old eds. *corb'd*) is "good," as Polonius would say; but I have no suspicion as to its meaning. It would be a pity to suggest an emendation.' Still, as Pandulpho is not meant to talk nonsense, I would suggest *coopèd*. Compare l. 144, 'Pish, thou canst not *coop* me up.'

The Malcontent, iv. 2. 112:—
 'Duke Pietro he banished for *banishing* his blood's dishonour.'

For *banishing*, I would read *publishing*. Pietro

has made known his wife's infidelity, but has not banished her.

The Malcontent, v. 1. 9 :—
Bilioso, 'an old choleric marshall,' is boasting of his prowess.

'When Monsieur Gundi lay here as ambassador, I could have carried a lady up and down at arm's end in a platter; and I can tell you, there were those at that time who, to try the strength of a man's back and his arm, would be *coistered*.'

Of *coistered* no other instance has been found in English literature. Reed suggests that the word may be derived from Old French *coisser = incommoder*, or *coiter = presser, exciter*. Nares thinks the meaning may be 'coiled up into a small compass.' Halliwell, *Dict. of Arch. and Prov. Words*, gives 'inconvenienced' (Fr.). But these seem unhappy guesses. Read *hoistered*, an Essex word meaning *supported, held up*, an extension of *hoisted*, as *hoisted* is of *hoised*.

The Malcontent, v. 2. 262 :—
'So 't be of *our* devising.'

Qy. 'of *soon* devising'? Compare l. 256 above, 'any *quick-done* fiction.'

The Malcontent, v. 2. 286 :—
'For no disastrous chance can ever move him,
That *leaveth* nothing but a God above him.'

Read *feareth*. Malevole is rejoicing at the turn

matters have taken, and encourages Celso to be of good heart.

The Malcontent, v. 3. 154 :—
> 'Speech to such, *ay*, O, what will affords !'

The line as it stands is to me unintelligible. Perhaps we should read,
> 'Speech to such *joy*, O,' etc.

i.e. there is no need for you to say 'no words,' for my joy is such that it chokes utterance. It may be noted by the way that the words, 'O my 'Altofront,' l. 150, are *extra metrum*.

The Dutch Courtezan, ii. 2. 214, 215 :—
> 'Yet man's but *man's* excrement—man breeding man,
> As he does worms, or this, to spoil this nothing.
>   [*He spits.*'

Perhaps,
> 'Yet man's but excrement—man breeding man,
> As he does worms, or this [*He spits*], to spoil this nothing.'

The Dutch Courtezan, iii. 1. 17 :—
> 'Soft skins save us! there was stub-bearded John-a-Stile with a *ployden's* face saluted me last day and struck his bristles through my lips.'

What is *ployden's*? Surely *hoyden's*.

The Dutch Courtezan, v. 2. 139 :—
> 'Come, come, turn not a *man of time* to make all ill
> Whose goodness you conceive not.'

'The text seems corrupt,' says Bullen. Read 'man *o' th'* time.'

The Fawn, ii. 1. 101:—

'*Nym.* That I am; and my beneficence shall show it.
'*Herc.* I know you are by that word beneficence, which only speaks of the future tense (shall *know* it).'

Read, shall *show* it.

The Fawn, ii. 1. 179:—

'What? we are mutually incorporated, turn'd into one another, *brued* together.'

Does this mean *brewed*, *i.e.* of one and the same brew?

The Fawn, ii. 1. 197:—

'to lie with one's brother's wedlock, O, my dear Herod, 'tis *vile* and uncommon lust.'

Bullen remarks, 'This must be a misprint. Should we read "royal"?'

Is 'vile and uncommon' anything else but a hendiadys for 'monstrously vile'?

The Fawn, ii. 1. 218:—

'Her afternoon's private nap is taken. I shall take her napping.'

Qy. 'I shall *not* take her napping'?

The Fawn, iii. 1. 151:—

'O, Fawn, 'tis a lady even above ambition; and like the vertical sun, that neither forceth others to cast shadows, nor can *others force or* shade her.'

Qy. 'nor can *others' force* shade her'?

The Fawn, iii. 1. 214 :—

'*Dul.* Because I love him ; and because he is virtuous I love to marry him.
'*Phil.* His virtues !
'*Dul.* Ay, with him, his virtues.
'*Phil.* Ay, with him ! alas, sweet princess, love or virtue are not of the essence of marriage !
'*Dul. I jest* upon your misunderstanding ! I'll maintain that wisdom in a woman is a most foolish quality.'

The first edition gives *I iest*, the second *A jest*, the third *I rest*. Perhaps, *Ay, pest*, or *A pest ; Ay*, as is well known, was of old commonly written *I*.

The Fawn, iii. 1. 254 :—

'No, let my wise, aged, learned, intelligent father,—that can *interpret* eyes, understand the language of birds, interpret the grumbling of dogs and the conference of cats, etc.'

For '*interpret* eyes' I think we should read '*penetrate* eyes,' the word *interpret* being caught from the line below.

The Fawn, iii. 1. 354 :—

'Why, I did know *you* feigned.'

Read, '*he* feigned'; comparing ll. 343, 351 above.

The Fawn, iv. 1. 133 :—

'Why, then, hath not the direction of Nature thought it just that customary coyness, old-fashions, terms of honour and of modesty, forsooth, all laid aside, they court *not* us, beseech *not* us rather, for sweets of love than we them?'

Omit *not* in both cases.

The Fawn, iv. 1. 397 :—

'Yet I hope a man of wit may prevent his own mishap or if he *can* prevent it,' etc.

Read, 'if he *can't* prevent,' etc.

The Fawn, v. 1. 213 :—

'A statute made in the five thousand four hundred threescore and three year of the easeful reign of the mighty potent Don Cupid, emperor of sighs and protestations, great king of kisses, archduke of dalliance, and sole *loved of her*, for the maintaining and relieving of his old soldiers, maim'd or disabled in love.'

The second edition gives 'sole loved of *him*.' Read, 'sole *lord* of *hymen*,' 'hymen' being often spelt 'himen.' Note the gradation of titles from 'emperor' to 'lord' and compare *What You Will*, iii. 3. 6-8 : 'Emperor of Cracks, Prince of Pages, Marquess of Mumchance, and *sole* Regent over a Bale of False Dice.' Both passages are founded upon *Love's Labour's Lost*, iii. 1. 182-188, in which nearly all the titles used by Marston are ascribed to Cupid :—

'This senior-junior, giant-dwarf, Dan Cupid :
Regent of love-rhymes, *lord* of folded arms,
The anointed sovereign of sighs and groans,
Liege of all loiterers and malcontents,
Dread *prince* of plackets, *king* of codpieces.
Sole imperator and great general
Of trotting paritors.'

As an instance of the converse change, we have

in Fletcher's *Elder Brother*, v. 2. 15, 'my *lord* Charles' for 'my *lov'd* Charles.'

The Fawn, v. 1. 406:—

'I remember when I was a young man, in my father's days, there were *four gallant spirits, for resolution*, as proper for body, as witty in discourse, as were any in Europe, nay, Europe had not such; I was one of them.'

Read, 'four *as* gallant spirits for resolution, as,' etc., omitting the comma after 'spirits.'

Sophonisba, i. 2. 12:—

'I hate these figures in locution,
These *about phases* forced by ceremony.'

Read, 'these *about-faces*': 'figures in locution' suggest to the speaker figures in dancing, or in military exercises in which 'faces about' was a common order.

Sophonisba, i. 2. 76:—

'Hannibal, our *ancor* is come back; thy slight,
Thy stratagem, to lead war into Rome
To quite ourselves, hath now taught desperate Rome
T'assail our Carthage: now the war is here.'

For *ancor* Bullen substitutes *rancour*, observing 'old eds. "ancor" an obvious misprint. The meaning is, Our rancorous hatred of the Romans has recoiled on our own heads.' But *ancor*, the older and more correct spelling of *anchor*, is undoubtedly sound, and the meaning is, 'the anchor to which our vessel of state trusted (*sc.* the stratagem of carrying the war into the enemy's country) has given way, has failed to take hold of the bottom.' Compare Camillo's words, *The Winter's Tale*, i. 2. 213, 214, in reference to the difficulty Leontes had in persuading Polixenes to stay :—

> 'You had much ado *to make his anchor hold*,
> When you cast out, *it still came home.*'

Sophonisba, i. 2. 83, 84 :—

'Desire, fear, and hope receive no bond
By whom, we in ourselves are never but beyond.'

Does this mean, 'Desire, fear, and hope, by whose agency, prompted by which, we are never within rational limits, but always out of our orbits, acknowledge no restraint'? If so, the comma after *whom* should be removed and placed after *never*. If not, I see no sense in the passage.

Sophonisba, i. 2. 169 :—

> ''Twas I lost the fight ;
> My choice vexed Syphax, enraged Syphax struck
> *Arm's fate* ; yet Sophonisba not repents.'

For *arm's fate* Bullen conjectures *arm'd hate*. I think *arm's fate*, or rather *arms' fate*, is sound, and the metaphor that of deciding the fate of arms by a sudden blow on the scale which held the fortune of the Carthaginians; with an allusion to Brennus.

Sophonisba, i. 2. 228 :—

> ' Nature made all the rest of thy fair sex
> As weak essays to *make thee* a pattern
> Of what can be in woman.'

Read, ' to make *of* thee a pattern.'

Sophonisba, ii. 2. 71 :—

> 'O my king,
> My uncle, father, captain, *O* over all.'

Omit *O* caught from the line above.

Sophonisba, iii. 1. 63 :—

> 'Zanthia, Zanthia!
> Thou art not foul, go to; some lords are oft
> So much in love with their known ladies' bodies
> That they oft love their *vailes*: hold, hold, thou'st find
> To faithful care kings' bounty hath no shore.'

Bullen reads, 'That they oft love their—vails: hold,' etc., and remarks, ' Old eds. "that they oft love their vailes: hold," etc. If the text is not corrupt, we must suppose that a sentence breaks off at the word "their." Marston is fond of employing the horrid figure aposiopesis. "Vails" is intelligible on the supposition that Syphax is feeing the waiting-women.' He is no doubt doing so, perhaps with kisses as well as money (else why the words 'thou art not foul'?), but the obvious correction, as it seems to me, is 'that they oft love their *maids*.' Compare Fletcher, *The Noble Gentleman*, iv. 2. 12, 'I love thee for thy lady's sake,' said by Longueville in love with Madam Mount-Marine to her maid Maria.

Sophonisba, iii. 1. 147 :—

'Close the vault's mouth lest we do *slip* in drink.'

Probably *sleep*: Vangue has just been given a 'carouse,' and is afraid of sleeping on his watch. A few lines lower he says, 'I am very sleepy.' Possibly, however, *slip* may mean, 'be guilty of carelessness,' 'be caught tripping.'

Sophonisba, iii. 2. 7-9 :—

'know, best of lords,
It is a happy being, breath well famed,
For which love sees these thus.'

Bullen says, 'The text is corrupt. "Sees *me* thus" (*i.e.* sees me grateful), "sees *the* thus" (*i.e.* incense), and "sees *this use*" (*i.e.* interest of thanks), are alike unsatisfactory.' Quite so. But I think the text is sound, and that the sense is, 'For whom love sees these, *sc. being* and *breath*, to be thus,' *sc. happy* and *well famed*. Compare above, ii. 1. 135-137 :—

'Nor are you vile
Because the gods foresee; for gods, not we,
See as things are; things are not as we see.'

Sophonisba, iii. 2. 73 :—

'Before then Syphax join,
With new-strength'd Carthage, or can once unwind
His tangled sense from out so wild *amaze*.'

Read, *a maze*: 'unwind' and 'tangled' show this, I think.

Sophonisba, v. 3. 36, 37 :—
> 'Help,—help to *bear*
> *Some* happiness, ye powers! I have joy to spare.'

Bullen reads *bar*, which he says the sense clearly requires. I would retain *bear*, the reading of the old editions, with the sense of bear some of the happiness which is too great a burden for him; or, if any change is necessary, would substitute *such* for *some*.

Sophonisba, v. 3. 89 :—
> 'How near was I unto *the curse of man. Joy!*'

Read, 'unto the curse of man—joy!' *i.e.*, to joy which is the curse of man.

What You Will, Induction, l. 106 :—
> 'I'll not stand it; *may* chance recoil, and *be not* stuffed with saltpetre.'

Probably, "*'t* may chance recoil and (*i.e.* an) *'t* be stuffed,' etc.

What You Will, Induction, l. 111 :—
> '*Phil.* Genteletza, the women will put me out.
> '*Dor.* And they strive to put thee out, do thou endeavour to put them.'

Read, 'to put them *in*.'

What You Will, Prologue, l. 15 :—
> 'That can as soon slight *of* as find a blemish.

Read, 'slight *off*.'

What You Will, i. 1. 102 :—

> ' 'Tis foully writ, slight wit, cross'd here and there,
> But where thou find'st a blot, there *fall* a tear.'

Read, I think, *fell*.

What You Will, i. 1. 119 :—

> 'I'll craze my brain,
> But I'll dissever *all*.   *Thy* hopes unite.'

Read, 'all thy hopes unite': *i.e.*, I will dissever all that your hopes unite.

What You Will, ii. 1. 51 :—

> 'Devote to mouldy customs of *hoary* eld.'

Qy. *hoar?*

What You Will, ii. 1. 149 :—

> 'Sits howling at deserts more *battle* fate.'

'If,' says Bullen, 'the text is not corrupt, "more battle fate" must mean "more prosperous fortune." *Battle* and *batful*, applied to land, had the meaning—*fertile*, fruitful.'

I would read, *better*.

What You Will, ii. 2. 45 :—

> 'Come on, you Nathaniel, say you, say you next ; not too fast ; say *tretably* : say.'

Bullen remarks, 'Chaucer has *tretable* in the sense of *tractable, well-disposed*; but that sense does not suit the present passage.'

The pedant is hearing his pupils say their

lessons, and after Nathaniel has repeated a line of the *Propria Quae Maribus*, he exclaims 'Faster! faster!'

Can *tretably* be a misprint for *trotably*, the pedant's translation of the Latin *pedetentim*?

What You Will, ii. 2. 90 :—

'*Facundius*, and elaborate elegance *make* your presence gracious in the eyes of your mistress.'

Read, '*Facundious* and elaborate elegance *makes*,' etc., and omit the comma.

What You Will, ii. 2. 134 :—

'They live and eat, and sleep, and drink and die,
And are not touched with recollections
Of things o'er past, or stagger'd *infant* doubts
Of things succeeding.'

Read, *in faint*.

What You Will, ii. 2. 160 :—

'Delight, my spaniel slept, whilst I *baus'd* leaves,
Toss'd o'er the dunces, pored on the old print
Of titled words, and still my spaniel slept.'

Bullen passes *baus'd* without a note. Halliwell explains it in his Dictionary as 'kissed,' as though from the Latin *basiare*.

Lampatho, the student, is enumerating his various studies; and I have no doubt we should read *brous'd*, an old spelling of *brows'd*, with a play upon leaves of trees and leaves of books.

B

What You Will, iii. 2. 16 :—

'Marry, since we were hung by the heels on the *bátch* of Sicily, to make a jail-delivery of the sea in our maws, 'tis just three months.'

Either *beach* should be printed, or a note should explain that *batch* is a corruption of *beatch*, an old spelling of *beach*.

What You Will, iii. 2. 93 :—

'The tailors, starchers, sempsters, *poulterers*.'

Read, *poulters*, as the word was commonly spelt.

What You Will, iii. 2. 117 :—

'*Sest*, I 'll to Celia.'

Probably, *Pest*; and so in iv. 1. 362.

What You Will, iv. 1. 96, 97 :—

'He capers the lascivious blood *about*
 Within heart-pants, *nor* leaps the eye *nor* lips;
 Prepare yourselves to kiss, for you must be kiss'd.'

Read,

'He capers, the lascivious blood *without*,
 Within heart-pants; *now* leaps the eye, *now* lips;' etc.

The reference is to the presumptuous lover, Laverdure, who is cock-a-hoop with the certainty of winning his mistress; and the meaning is, 'he frisks about in his exultation, the glow of anticipated triumph causing his cheeks to burn, his heart beating wildly in his breast, his eyes and lips betraying ecstasy at the thought of the amorous encounter at hand.'

What You Will, iv. 1. 127 :—

> 'by this light the dull-ey'd thinks he does well, does very well.'

After *dull-ey'd*, qy. should we not insert *fool*?

What You Will, iv. 1. 140-146 :—

> '*Lamp*. Bless you, fair ladies ! God make you all his servants !
> '*Meletza*. God make you all his servants !
> '*Quadra*. He is holpen well had need of you; for be it spoken without profanism, he hath more in his train. I fear me you ha' more servants than he : I am sure the devil is an angel of darkness.'

This, as it stands, seems to me stark nonsense. I would therefore read, ' For, be it spoken without profanism, *if* he hath more in his train, I fear me you have more servants than he,' etc., with the meaning, ' He (*sc.* God), who has many nominal attendants (*is holpen well*), needs you sadly; for, if I may say so without profanity, if he has more who nominally follow in his train, I fear you have more devoted servants, and among those servants I may reckon the devil, who, as an angel of darkness, is well suited to your service.' In *servants* there is, of course, an allusion to the old sense of devoted admirers.

What You Will, iv. 1. 181, 182:—

The student, Lampatho, abjures all study.

> Lamp-oil, watch-candles, rug-gowns and small juice,
> Thin commons, four o'clock rising,—I renounce you all.
> Now *may I'ternally abandon* meat,
> Rust, fusty, you *which* most *embraced* disuse,
> You ha' made me an ass.'

Read,

> 'Now *my eternally abandon'd* meat,
> Rust fusty you *with* most *enforced* disuse.'

What You Will, iv. 1. 238, 241:—

> '*Were* not a pleasing jest for me to clothe
> Another rascal like Albano, say,
> And rumour him return'd, without all deceit?
> *Would* not beget errors most ridiculous?'

Read, '*Were't*,' and '*Would't*.'

Eastward Ho, iv. 1. 43:—

> 'Poor man, how weak he is! the *weak* water has wasted away his strength.'

The second *weak* should, I think, be omitted; and perhaps we should read *washed* for *wasted*.

The Insatiate Countess, i. 1. 97:—

> 'You're virtuous, man; nay, let me not blush to say so.'

This, Bullen's reading, seems to me pointless. The edition of 1613 gives, 'your vertues *man*'; that of 1631, 'Your vertues *may*.'

Conjectural Readings 21

Read, I think,

'Your virtues *wan me*; let me not blush to say so.'

Compare Fletcher, *The Custom of the Country*, iii. 2, where the equally 'insatiate' Hippolyta solicits the obdurate Arnaldo.

'You make me fonder:
You have a virtuous mind; I want that ornament.'

And Dekker, *The Honest Whore*, vol. ii. p. 39, Pearson's Reprint,

'For thou then destroy'st
That which I love thee for, thy virtues,'

said by Bellafronte, the Honest Whore, to Hippolito.

The Insatiate Countess, i. 1. 108 :—

'That *fame-insatiate* devil jealousy.'

Read,

'That *same insatiate* devil, jealousy.'

The Insatiate Countess, ii. 2. 28-34 :—

'You are the party, I perceive, and here's a white sheet that your husband has promised me to do penance in . . . though there be not such rare phrases in 't [*sc.* as in that from her husband to Thais], 'tis more to the matter : a legible hand, but for the dash or the (he) and (as): short bawdy parentheses as ever you saw, to the purpose.'

Abigail is showing to her friend, Thais, an insulting love-letter which she has received from that friend's husband; Thais having just before shown one written in very high-flown terms which she has received from Abigail's husband. Bullen notes, 'I follow the reading of the old copies.' But that reading is free from all suspicion, except that perhaps there should be a comma rather than a colon after (*as*). The *dash* is the mark of a break, and the (*he*) and (*as*) are the brackets used in omissions for decency sake, the *short bawdy parentheses* she goes on to mention, (*he*) and (*as*), indicating the monosyllabic character of the words omitted. Such parentheses are not infrequent in the old dramatists, and we have an instance of one in *The Malcontent*, v. 2. 4 :—

> 'The Dutchman for a drunkard,—
> The Dane for golden locks,—
> The Irishman for usquebaugh,—
> The Frenchman for the (   ).'

The Insatiate Countess, iii. 2. 7 :—

'Fear *keep* with cowards, *air-stars* cannot move.'

Read,

'Fear *keeps* with cowards, *air stars* cannot move' :

i.e. fear dwells with cowards, such an airy nothing cannot move fixed stars like ourselves. So, a few lines lower, after arguing the matter, Massino says, 'Madam, I yield to you, fear *keeps with love.*' For *move* compare *The Malcontent*, v. 2. 285.

Conjectural Readings 23

The Insatiate Countess, iii. 2. 46 :—

> 'Nature did rob herself when she made him,
> Blushing to see her work excel herself;
> 'Tis shape makes mankind *femelacy*.'

Perhaps,

> ''Tis shape makes mankind*'s simulacracy*,'

i.e. it is form that makes men worshipped as though they were idols. Compare *The Widow*, i. 1, 'Now as he stands he's worth a woman's love'; and *The Laws of Candy*, ii. 1., 'Carriage and state *makes us seem demi-gods*.'

The Insatiate Countess, iii. 4. 52 :—

> 'My love was dotage till I loved thee,
> For thy soul truly tastes our petulance;
> *Condition's* lover, Cupid's intelligencer.'

Read, I think,

> '*Coition's* lover, Cupid's intelligencer.'

The Insatiate One speaks of 'petulance,' *i.e.* a provoking coyness, as Coition's bosom-lover, arch-confederate, Cupid's go-between. Compare above, iii. 2. 100-112.

The Insatiate Countess, iii. 4. 96 :—

> 'Never to seek *weaking* variety.'

Read,

> 'Never to seek *wasting* variety.'

Commenting upon Swynfen Jervis's conjecture

wakefull couche for *wastefull cocke*, *Timon of Athens*, ii. 2. 171, Ingleby, *The Still Lion*, p. 117, remarks, 'In the "upper case" of the compositor the ſt and k are in contiguous "boxes," so that an ſt would sometimes be dropped into the k box by mistake . . . whence it might well happen that *wakefull* was set up for *wastefull*.' This accident has, I think, happened here; for Marston, rugged as he is, would scarcely have written anything so cacophonous as 'seek weaking.' For an instance of the converse, compare Heywood's *Silver Age*, ii. 1 :—

'Whose powerful arm gave strength unto my lord
To *worst* his safety through these dangerous wars:'

where we should read *work*.

The Insatiate Countess, iv. 2. 66 :—

'Her *quenchless* lust has quite benumbed my knowledge.'

This, the conjecture of the editor of 1820, is retained by Bullen. The old editions give *vselesse*, which it seems to me could not have been a corruption of *quenchlesse*. Read *cureless*, *i.e.* incurable; and compare *The Rape of Lucrece*, l. 772, 'Since thou art guilty of my *cureless* crime'; *The Merchant of Venice*, iv. 1. 142, 'Repair thy wit, good youth, or it will fall To *cureless* ruin'; Fletcher, *Monsieur Thomas*, iii. 1, 'In all thy course's *cureless* disobedience'; and *Thierry and Theodoret*, v. 2, 'this *cureless* malice.'

The Insatiate Countess, iv. 5. 17 :—

> 'Bawds to lust and murder,
> Be all propitious to my act of justice
> Upon the scandalizer of her fame,
> That is the life-blood of deliciousness,
> *Deem'd* Isabella, Cupid's treasurer,
> Whose soul contains the richest gifts of love.'

Qy. '*queen'd* Isabella,' *i.e.* queen-like? Somewhat similar is '*kingdom'd* Achilles,' *Troilus and Cressida*, ii. 3. 185, and the dramatists abound in adjectives formed from nouns, and often mistaken for participles. Bullen proposes *dear* or *divine*, both of which seem equally tame, especially in Don Sago's mouth, while it is improbable that even the perverse ingenuity of copyist or compositor should have substituted *deem'd* for either of such ordinary words. *Queen'd* would be a word unfamiliar to them, and they might easily substitute *Deem'd*, which was of common use.

The Insatiate Countess, iv. 5. 22 :—

> '*Sago.* Who's there?
> '*Massino.* A friend to thee, if thy intents
> Be just and honourable.
> '*Sago.* Count Massino, speak, I am the watch.
> '*Massino.* My name is Massino: dost thou know me?
> '*Sago.* Yes, slanderous villain,' etc.

I believe the words *Count Massino* should be omitted. That Sago does not recognise Massino, till he declares himself, is evident from the words 'I am the watch,' which Sago uses in order to make Massino give his name; for, upon his doing so, Sago at once fiercely attacks him with every epithet of vituperation, and declares his intention of killing him. It is no objection to this that upon Massino's asking, 'Dost thou know me?' Sago replies, 'Yes,' for he merely means that he knows Massino from what Isabella had said of him. Note that by omitting the words *Count Massino* the metre of the line becomes perfect; also that there is certainly corruption in the passage since the old editions give 'Rogero' for 'Massino,' and prefix 'Rog.' to his speeches here.

The Insatiate Countess, v. 1. 4 :—

'Don Sago, quakest thou not to behold this spectacle—
This innocent sacrifice, murder'd nobleness—
When blood, the Maker ever promiseth,
Shall though with slow, yet with sure vengeance *rest*?'

For *rest* read *rise*. The corpse of Massino, murdered by Sago, has just been brought in, and the allusion is to *Genesis*, iv. 10, 'The voice of thy brother's blood crieth unto Me from the ground.'

The Insatiate Countess, v. 1. 42 :—

'What Tanais, Nilus, or what Tigris swift,
What Rhenus ferier than the cataract,—
Although *Neptolis cold, the waves of all the Northern Sea*
Should flow for ever through these guilty hands,
Yet the sanguinolent stain should extant be.'

Read,

'Although, *Niphates-cold, the Northern Sea*,' etc.,

i.e. though the Northern Sea, as cold as Mount Niphates, should flow, etc. I imagine that Marston originally wrote, 'Although the waves of all the Northern Sea,' etc., that he then, in order to intensify the idea by a comparison with the Snow Mountain, inserted the words 'Niphates-cold' (which the compositor corrupted into 'Neptolis cold'), and that he either forgot to strike out the words 'the waves of all,' or that the compositor did not notice that they had been struck out. Note that 'Neptolis,' if there were such a word, would be accented on the first syllable, whereas we require a word, like 'Niphates,' accented on the second syllable. Don Sago is very fond of classical allusions, and in his 'Ercles' vein' would be likely to drag in one to Mount Niphates. Bullen proposes, 'Though Neptune cold,' but this seems unbearably tame, and Sago would at least have said 'Neptunus.' Marston was a classical scholar; had he in his mind *Oedipus Tyrannus*, 1227, 1228,

οἶμαι γὰρ οὔτ' ἂν Ἴστρον οὔτε Φᾶσιν ἂν
νίψαι καθαρμῷ τήνδε τὴν στέγην.

The Scourge of Villainy, i. 2. 135 :—

'When tenure for short years (by many a one)
Is thought right good be turn'd *forth* Littleton,
All to be heady, or freehold at least,
When it is all one, for long time be a beast,
A slave, as have a short term'd tenancy.'

Read and punctuate as follows:—

> 'When tenure for short years, by many a one
> Is thought right good be turn'd (*fourth* Littleton)
> All to be heady, or freehold at least;
> When it is all one for long life be a beast,
> A slave, as have a short term'd tenancy.'

The meaning being, 'when by many it is thought right good that tenure for a short term should be converted into tenure *in capite*, or freehold tenure at least; when it is thought that to have a short tenure (*i.e.* anything less than a tenure *in capite*, or a freehold tenure) is no better than to be a beast or a slave for long life.' There is an evident allusion to Littleton's Tenures, and '*forth* Littleton,' *i.e.* '*fourth* Littleton,' I take to be a jocose reference to an apocryphal fourth book (there are only three), as who should say, by way of hoax, 'see *Iliad* bk. xxv.,' or '*Genesis*, chap. li.,' the form of reference being in imitation of that to statutes, as we say, 'iv. Vict.' etc., or, as they said of old, 'quarto Edw.' etc. Compare *The Staple of News*, iv. 1, 'Thou shalt read All Littleton's Tenures to me'; and, for the form of citation, *The Queen of Corinth*, v. 4, 'Lycurgus the nineteenth against rapes.'

The Scourge of Villainy, iii. 11. 33:—

> 'A hall, a hall!
> Room for the spheres, the orbs celestial
> Will dance Kempe's Jig; they'll revel with neat jumps;
> A worthy poet has put on their pumps.

> O *wit's* quick traverse, but *sance ceo's* slow ;
> Good faith, 'tis hard for nimble Curio.
> Ye gracious orbs, keep the old measuring ;
> All's spoil'd if once ye fall to capering.'

Among the objects of this satire is one Curio, whose aim and occupation in life is dancing. After describing his fantastic behaviour, the poet imagines a dance of the spheres, as in the *Rehearsal* 'the earth, sun, and moon come out upon the stage and dance the Hay.' The clumsy efforts of the 'celestial orbs' to show their agility irritate the 'nimble Curio,' and he begs them to return to their former stately manner of moving, the 'measure' of old days, and not attempt to rival him in capering.

Read therefore,

> 'O *wits* quick traverse, but *san cielo's* slow ;'

i.e. poets are nimble enough in their imagination, but holy heaven (the 'celestial orbs') cannot keep pace with such thoughts. The word 'traverse' was formerly used for 'moving the feet with proportion, as in dancing,' as well as for 'marching'; compare *e.g.*, Heywood, *A Woman Killed with Kindness*, i. 2, 'Jack Slime, *traverse* you with Cicely Milkpail.'

The Scourge of Villainy, iii. 11. 54 :—

> 'Of counter times, *finctures*, sly passatas.

Read *fincturas* ; pluralising the Italian form, as

in *passatas*. Murray, *Eng. Dict.*, quotes Saviolo, *Practice*, H. iv. a, 'If he use any *fincture* or false thrust, answer him not'; and gives the Italian *finctura*, modern *fintura*. Bullen therefore is right in explaining the word as 'feints.'

II. BEAUMONT AND FLETCHER.[1]

Thierry and Theodoret, i. 1. vol. i. p. 109:—

'I do but gently tell you what becomes you,
  And what may bend your honour; how these courses
  Of loose and lazy pleasures, not suspected,
  But done and known; your mind that knows no limit
  (And all your actions *follow*), which *loose* people,
  That see but through a mist of circumstance,
  Dare term ambitious.'

For *follow* the old editions give *follows*; I would read *fellows*. I also suspect *loose* in l. 5 of the extract, the word apparently having been caught from the line but one above.

Thierry and Theodoret, i. 1. vol. i. p. 111:—

'And by a rush that one day's warmth
  Hath shot up to this swelling.'

Qy. 'one day's *sudden* warmth'? compare *The Princess*, v. 292,

'in her a Jonah's gourd
  Up in one night, and due to *sudden* sun.'

Thierry and Theodoret, i. 1. vol. i. p. 111:—

'Bless us!
  For now I do begin to feel myself
  Turning into a halter, and the ladder
  Turning from me, one pulling at my legs too.'

---

[1] The references are to Dyce's edition, eleven vols., 1843-1846.

Qy. *girning, i.e.* grinning? Compare *The Lovers' Progress,* v. 3,

> 'I ever had
> A hanging look; and a wise woman told me,
> Though I had not the heart to do a deed
> Worthy the halter, in my youth or age
> I should take a turn *with a wry mouth.*'

Thierry and Theodoret, iii. 1. vol. i. p. 149 :—

> 'The best of men in full ability
> Can only hope to satisfy a wife;
> And for that hope ridiculous, I in my want,
> And such defective poverty, that to her bed
> From my first cradle brought no strength but thought,
> Have met a temperance beyond her's that rock'd me,
> Necessity being her bar; where this
> Is so much senseless of my depriv'd fire,
> She knows it not a loss by her desire.'

Dyce notes, ' Mason proposed to read, "*as* my first cradle," *i.e. as to my first cradle*, the particle *to* referring to *cradle* as well as to *bed* in the preceding line : with this amendment the passage requires no explanation. *That rocked* here means that nursed me." This conjecture was adopted by Weber, who, however, allows that " the word *from* was not easily corrupted into *as*."'

I believe there is no corruption here, but take the construction, harsh as it is, to be 'in my want and that defective poverty (inherent in me) from my first cradle which brought,' etc. The sense will then be, And as regards such hope, I, made ridiculous by that congenital impotence which brought to her bed only the will and not the power to satisfy a wife, have found in her a temperance beyond that of my nurse, in whose case it (her temperance) was a matter of necessity, whereas in the case of my wife no looseness of desire makes her conscious of my deficiency.

Thierry and Theodoret, v. 2. vol. i. p. 189 :—
> 'Yet I must crave
> That feed ye and protect ye and *proclaim* ye.'

Qy. *maintain*, the prefix *pro*— being caught from *protect*?

Philaster, i. 1. vol. i. p. 218 :—

'Do but view yon stranger well, and you shall see a fever through all his bravery, and feel him shake like a *true tenant*; if he give not back his crown again upon the report of an elder-gun, I have no augury.'

Dyce notes, 'So all the old editions, except 4to 1620, which has "true *truant*." Theobald printed, "true *recreant*"; and so his successors. I am not satisfied that "tenant" is the right reading; but I am far from thinking with Theobald that "it is as arrant nonsense as ever the press was guilty of"; see what immediately follows: "if he [shaking like a true tenant—like one who has only a temporary possession] *give not back* his crown." etc. The Rev. J. Mitford conjectures "true *tyrant*."'

With Theobald I regard 'true tenant,' as arrant nonsense, and suggest *trutinant*, *i.e.* a pair of scales. 'Trutinate' and 'trutination' are not uncommon, and 'trutinant' is an easy coinage on the analogy of a 'ruminant,' a 'variant,' an 'esculent.'

The Maid's Tragedy, i. 2. vol. i. p. 338 :—

'*Nept.* Great queen of us and heaven, hear what I bring
To make this hour a full one, *if not her measure.*
Cynth. Speak, sea's king.'

The passage, says Dyce, ' stands thus in the old editions,

"Great queen of us and heaven,
  Hear what I bring to make this hour a full one,
  If not her measure."

'The words " if not her measure " were thrown out of the text by Theobald, and, as far as the metre is concerned, it was certainly an improvement. "Some careful annotator," he says, "had made a marginal *quære* at the close of the second song, *if not her measure, i.e.* whether this measure is not to be sung by Cynthia; as it undoubtedly is: but the note of reference to this *quære* being forgot, it was mistaken at press for a part of the text and casually clapt to Neptune's speech." Theobald had forgotten that *measure* meant a dance, not a song; and, if we suppose that the words in question are not a portion of the text, the probability would be that they are a corruption of " If not, here measure," *i.e.* if the present speech and the two next speeches (none of which are found in the 4to 1619) be omitted by the actors, let the measure be danced here. In the Postscript to vol. i. of ed. of 1750, Seward proposed to read, "If not, *o'er*-measure"; and observes, "as to the interruption of the measure [*i.e.* metre] such intercalations of words between verses are used by our authors. Thus [in *The Faithful Shepherdess*, towards the end of the last act],

> "We have perform'd a work
> Worthy the gods themselves.
> *Sat.* Come forward, maiden; do not lurk,"

the hemistich is an intercalation; the liberties in measure taken by our old dramatic poets being quite boundless." The edition of 1778 and Weber adopted Seward's needless alteration, "o'er-measure." The meaning of Neptune's speech is clearly this: Great queen of us and heaven, hear what I bring, endeavouring to make this hour a full one, though perhaps what I bring may not completely fill up her measure. The pronoun *her* is frequently applied to *hour* by our early writers.'

That Dyce of all critics should offer such an explanation is to me astounding. I believe that the words are a stage direction to come after the second song, and that for '*if not her* measure,' we should read '*another* measure' (*if* being misread for *a*): each song will then have its own 'measure,' as in the case of the four songs in the *Masque of the Inner Temple*. And the passage will run,

> '*Nept.* Great queen of us and heaven, hear what I bring
> To make this hour a full one.
> *Cynth.* Speak, sea's King.'

Seward's remark as to the passage in *The Faithful Shepherdess* is hardly to the point, for there the metre changes from decasyllabics in the one speech to octosyllabics in the other. Here the masque, except for the songs, is throughout in one metre, and is remarkable for its perfect rhythm.

The Maid's Tragedy, ii. 2. vol. i. p. 359 :—

' I have done, sit down ; and let us
  Upon that point fix all our eyes, that point there.
  Make a dull silence, till *you feel a sudden* sadness
  Give us new souls.'

Theobald rejects *sudden*. Rather reject *you feel*. The poet had written 'till you feel a sadness'; he then changed it to 'till a sudden sadness,' for two reasons. First that the thought is thus made more vivid and poetical; secondly, that 'till *you* feel a sadness give *us* new souls' is illogical and scarcely grammatical.

The Faithful Shepherdess, i. 1. vol. ii. p. 26 :—

' Nuts more brown
Than the squirrel's teeth that crack them.'

Here in opposition to Seward's remark that 'the teeth of the squirrel is the only visible part that is not brown,'—a remark not wholly accurate, Weber cites from Herrick's *Oberon's Feast*,

'The red capp'd worm, that's shut
Within the concave of a *nut*
Brown as his tooth.'

But the quotation is in no wise apposite, for Herrick is stating an actual fact, the mandibles of the worm being brown; whereas here we have nothing to do with brown teeth, the words of the text meaning only 'nuts more brown than the squirrel whose teeth crack them,'—an inversion which it is strange the various editors should not have seen.

The Faithful Shepherdess, ii. 2. vol. ii, pp. 48, 49:—

> 'Thou blessèd star, I thank thee for thy light,
> Thou by whose power the darkness of sad night
> Is banish'd from the earth, in whose dull place
> Thy chaster beams play on the heavy face
> Of all the world, making the blue sea smile,
> To see how cunningly thou dost beguile
> Thy brother of his brightness, giving day
> Again from chaos; whiter than that way
> That leads to Jove's high court, and chaster far
> Than chastity itself, *you blessèd star*
> *That nightly shines. Thou all the constancy*
> That in all women was or e'er shall be;
> From whose fair eye-balls flies that holy fire.
> That poets style the mother of desire,
> Infusing into every gentle breast
> A soul of greater price, and far more blest,
> Than that quick power which gives a difference
> 'Twixt man and creatures of a lower sense.'

'So,' says Dyce, 'the two earliest quartos, except that the first has "*brightly* shines." Later editions, "*you* blessèd," etc. Seward printed,

> "*Thou* blessed star
> That nightly shin'*st*";

'So the editors of 1778; and so Weber, except that he gave "shines." This speech is a very obscure one. That part of it is addressed to the moon (see the eleventh line [*i.e.* l. 7 of my extract]), "Thy brother," etc., is not be doubted. Qy. in the present passage is "*yon* blessèd star," the right reading, and does Thenot begin to address Clorin at "whiter than that way," proceeding to call her chaster than the goddess of chastity, "*yon* blessèd star," *i.e.* the moon, which he had so termed in the fourth [*i.e.* l. 1 of my extract] line of the speech, "Thou blessèd star, I thank thee," etc. ?'

Before giving my conjecture, I will state the objections I feel to the reading in Dyce's edition. (1) The change in the person apostrophised, if there is a change, is very abrupt, and *whiter* is a strange epithet to apply to Clorin; (2) except in '*you* blessèd star (l. 10 of the extract) the second person singular is used throughout; (3) 'that nightly shines,' to say nothing of the grammar, is contrary to fact, and has no pertinence here: (4) 'Thou all the constancy,' etc., is a very awkward construction of doubtful sense. Taking, then, the reading of the first quarto *brightly*, and substituting *thou* for *you* (in l. 10), I suggest that the lines should run:—

'*Thou* blessèd star
That *brightly out*shin'*st* all the constancy,' etc.

It may be objected that the moon was by no means an emblem of constancy; but from the words 'thy chaster beams,' and 'thy brother,' it seems to me that here Fletcher was especially thinking of the moon *as representing Diana*, the goddess of chastity (and the sun as representing Phoebus).

The Faithful Shepherdess, ii. 3. vol. ii. p. 55 :—

> 'This holy well, my grandame that is dead,
>   Right wise in charms, hath often to me said,
>   Hath power to change the form of any creature,
>   Being thrice dipp'd o'er the head, into what feature
>   Or shape 'twould please the letter-down to crave,
>   Who must pronounce this charm too, which she gave
>   [*Showing a scroll.*
>   Me on her death-bed ; told me what, and how,
>   I should apply it to the patient's brow
>   That would be *chang'd, casting them thrice asleep*
>   Before I trusted them into this deep.'

Read,

> 'That would be *changèd, casting them asleep.*'

Nothing is said about casting them *thrice* asleep (which, in fact, would be almost nonsense), but the word *thrice* has crept in from l. 4, 'Being *thrice* dipp'd'; see below :—

> 'Come, my temples bind
>   With these sad herbs, and when I sleep, you find,
>   As you do speak, *thrice down me let,*
>   And bid the water raise me Amoret.'

So, ii. 1. 1-6 :—

> 'From thy forehead thus I take
>   These herbs, and charge thee not awake
>   Till in yonder holy well
>   *Thrice*, with powerful magic spell
>   Fill'd with many a baleful word,
>   Thou hast been dipp'd.'

Note, too, the rhythm of the whole passage down to the end of the scene as being opposed to the reading in the text.

The Faithful Shepherdess, iii. 1. vol. ii. p. 64:—

> 'She was alone
> With me; if then her presence did so move
> Why did I not assay to win her love?
> She would *not* sure have yielded unto me;
> Women love only opportunity,
> And not the men; or if she had denied,
> Alone I might have forc'd her to have tried
> Who had been stronger: oh, vain fool, to let
> Such bless'd occasion pass.'

Read,

> 'She would *most* sure have yielded.'

The whole context, especially the alternative '*or* if she had denied,' shows this, and *not* has been caught from the line above.[1]

The Honest Man's Fortune, i. 1. vol. ii. p. 345:—

> '*Sec. Law.* Courage! you have the law.
> *Long.* And you the *profit*.'

Dyce's reading, that of the MS., is *profit*. Both the folios give *profits*; and rightly, I think, for this reason. A few speeches above (p. 344) Dubois says, 'He is but his brother-in-law,' and

---

[1] Curiously enough, a day or two after correcting the first proof, I found in Mortimer Collins's novel *A Fight with Fortune*, ii. 65, a precisely similar misprint: 'And dreams have *not* power over us when the vital power is not at its highest; then they come, often in a refreshing, but often also in a torturing form'; the two *nots*, as here, being exactly over and under each other in two lines of printing.

Conjectural Readings

Longueville punningly answers, 'Law! that's as bad.' So here, I feel sure, he is punning upon the biblical expression 'the law and the *prophets*.'

Cupid's Revenge, i. 1. vol. ii. p. 363 :—

> 'If younger sisters
> Take not the greater charity, 'tis lawful.'

Qy. '*as 'tis* lawful'?

Cupid's Revenge, ii. 2. vol. ii. p. 378 :—

> 'That I *am* a widow, full of tears in show,
> (My husband dead, and one that lov'd me so,
> Hardly a week) forgot my modesty,' etc.

I would omit *am*, which does not improve the metre, while it involves an unnecessary ellipsis of the relative.

Cupid's Revenge, ii. 6. vol. ii. p. 393 :—

> 'Now Heaven defend me!
> Your whore *you shall* never. I thank the gods I have
> A little left to keep me warm and honest :
> If your grace take not that, I seek no more.'

Dyce notes, 'The two earliest 4tos, and the folio of 1679, have "your whore shall never." The 4to of 1635 has the reading which I have adopted, and which (though I hardly think it can be the genuine one) may mean: "Your whore you shall never *win me to be*." Seward printed, "Your whore? you shall never ——," marking it as a broken sentence ; and so Weber.'

Qy. 'Your whore, *sir*, never'?

Cupid's Revenge, v. 4. vol. ii. p. 441 :—

> ' I cannot tell ;
> If I go from you, sir, *I shall ne'er dawn day more.*'

Seward and the editors of 1778 print *draw* for *dawn*. I would read, ' I'll ne'er *see day dawn more,*' comparing her words above v. i. p. 437, ' Why, an I do, would *I might ne'er see day again.*'

Urania uses provincialisms, but does not misuse speech. Cp. also *The Woman's Prize*, vol. vii. p. 163.

Four Plays in One: The Triumph of Honour, Sc. i. vol. ii. p. 490 :—

> ' Valerius,
> 'Tis less dishonour to thee thus to kill me
> Than bid me kneel to Martius ; 'tis to murder
> The fame of living men, which great men do ;
> Their studies strangle ; poison makes away,
> The wretched hangman only ends the play.'

Seward writes, ' By making the first part of the sentence end at *strangle*, the following sense may be deduced from it. To make their fellow-creatures kneel to them, as great men frequently do, is worse than murdering them ; it renders them servile and slavish, debases them below the dignity of their nature, murders therefore their fame, and fetters and strangles their *studies*, *i.e.* the free exertions of their rational faculties. Whereas poison makes away or destroys a man without injuring his fame or diminishing the dignity of his soul ; and the wretched despicable hangman only puts an end to the part we act upon the stage of this world. The sentiment is

Conjectural Readings 43

continued and improved in Sophocles's next speech upon death.' The editors of 1778 remark, ' Probably we should point,

> " Which great ones do
> Their studies strangle."

The sense is, You will dishonour me less by killing me than by bidding me kneel to Martius. Great men exert themselves to murder the fame of the living; which is greater cruelty than poison or hanging, which but concludes our misery.' Mason, ' I should read,

> "'Tis to murder
> The fame of living men, *when* great ones do
> Their studies strangle," etc.,

and the meaning may possibly be this: that when great men, by their power, force others to depart from the principles they have formed from their studies, they destroy their fame.' Weber adopted the alteration proposed by Mason. Dyce ' amid so much uncertainty ' prefers ' following the old eds.'

None of the above readings or explanations at all commend themselves to me. I feel convinced we should read,

> ' Their studies *strangling* poison makes away,'

with the meaning that the suffocating poison of dishonour utterly distroys the noble objects for which they have lived, while the executioner merely puts an end to their lives. The word *only* indicates an emphatic antithesis between *studies* used (as often in the old dramatists) in the technical sense of the part which the actor has to study, and the *play* itself, *i.e.* the player's action on the stage of life. The former would endure if calumny did not destroy them, though the latter might have come to an end. The consequent antithesis between the effect of poison, *i.e.* poisonous dishonour, and the hangman's action is completely slurred over by Mason and the editors of 1778.

For the sentiment, compare *The Triumph of Fame*, sc. i. vol. ii. p. 510,

'Wouldst have me murder thee beyond thy death?
Unjustly scandal thee with ravishment?'

So, *The Laws of Candy*, i. 2. vol. v. p. 326:—

''Tis a cruelty
More than to murder innocents, to take
The life of my yet-infant honour from me';

and *Valentinian*, iv. 4. vol. v. p. 283:—

'See my poor body burnt, and some to sing
About my pile, and what I have done and suffer'd,
If Cæsar kill not that too.'

For *strangle*, in the sense of suffocate, compare *Romeo and Juliet*, iv. 3. 35:—

'Shall I not then be stifled in the vault
. . . . .
And there lie *strangled* ere my Romeo comes?'

Also Marston, ii. *Antonio and Mellida*, i. 172:—

'That I should drop strong *poison* in the bowl, . . .
That it should work even in the hush of night,
And *strangle* him on sudden.'

In the present passage the word is figuratively used in contrast with the physical strangling by the hangman's rope.

Four Plays in One: The Triumph of Honour, sc. ii. vol. ii. p. 499 :—

> 'When men shall read the records of thy valour,
> Thy hitherto-brave virtue, and approach
> (Highly content yet) to *this* foul assault
> Included in this leaf, this ominous leaf,
> They shall throw down the book, and read no more,
> Though the best deeds ensue, and all conclude
> That ravelled the whole story, whose sound heart
> (Which should have been) prov'd the most leprous part.'

'Heath,' says Dyce '(MS. notes), conjectures "*Thou'st* ravell'd the whole story." Mason proposed to read, "That ravell'd *thy* whole story," an alteration which Weber adopted. The text may be corrupted; but passages which can hardly be reconciled to grammar occur elsewhere in these plays.'

I do not think any emendation is called for, except that '*the* foul' would be an improvement upon '*this* foul,' and that possibly *ravelled* should be *travelled*. In the two last lines of the passage there is a plethora of relatives, and a confusion of constructions between 'he whose heart should have been sound, proved leprous in that part,' and 'his heart which should have been sound proved the most leprous part.' In *The Queen of Corinth*, iv. 3. vol. v. p. 464, there is a closely parallel passage :—

> 'But yet remember, when posterity
> Shall read your volumes fill'd with virtuous acts,
> And shall arrive at this black bloody leaf,
> Noting your foolish barbarism, and my wrong
> (As time shall make it plain), what follows this,
> Decyphering any noble deed of yours,
> Shall be quite lost, for men will read no more.'

Here the words 'shall arrive ... leaf' perhaps confirm my suggestion *travelled*, while, on the other hand, 'decyphering' may support *ravelled*. There is also perhaps in the two last lines a similar confusion of constructions.

Four Plays in One: The Triumph of Death, sc. iv. vol. ii. p. 552:—

> 'Hang thee,
> Base bigamist, *thou honour of ill* women.'

Dyce notes, 'Altered by Seward to " thou *horror* of *all* women." "Seward's alteration, which Mr. Mason wishes [is "rather inclined"] to restore, is very tame, and, what is more, incorrect, for Lavall is far from being detested by *all* women."— WEBER.'

Read without doubt,

> 'Hang thee!
> Base bigamist thou, *dis*honour of *all* women';

comparing p. 558,

> 'Nay, out it shall; there take his false heart to ye,
>   [*Throwing down Lavall's heart.*
> The *base dishonour of a thousand women.*'

Four Plays in One: The Triumph of Death, sc. v. vol. ii. p. 554 :—

> '*Law.* Now I am bravely quarried.
> *Per.* 'Tis my sister.
> *Gab.* No, bawdy slave, no treacher, she is not *carried*.'

Qy. *quarried*? *i.e.* provided as your prey.

The Scornful Lady, ii. 3. vol. iii. p. 44 :—

> 'Go, thou art a pretty *fore*-handed fellow!'

Qy. *free*-handed?

The Coxcomb, ii. 2. vol. iii. p. 152 :—

> ''Twill be a black time with you else; sheathe your *bung* whore.'

No doubt *bung* was frequently used for a purse, but we have no authority for its being used for the knife with which a purse was cut; I would therefore read '*bung-nipper*.'

The Coxcomb, ii. 3. vol. iii. p. 157 :—

> '*Maria.* What's he would speak with me?
> *Serv.* A Kilkenny *ring*;
> There he stands, madam.'

Weber conjectures that the right reading is *rung*, which in Scotland signifies a coarse heavy staff: Dyce, in his *Addenda et Corrigenda*, vol. i. p. cxiv. says, 'No alteration is required. In *Looke About You*, 1600, we find: "Cauilero Skinke being beleagerd with an hoste of leaden heeles arm'd in *ring* Irish, cheated my hammerer of his Red cap and coate," etc., Sig. L.'

Read, 'A Kilkenny *rug*,' *i.e.* a rough-headed fellow. So p. 159, Maria addresses him as, 'Sirra *Thatch'd head*,' 'you *Hobby-headed* rascal,' in which latter expression the epithet, as Weber points out, refers to the high-platted hair of the Irish wood-kern, hanging over his eyes, the substantive 'hobby' to the Irish hobby or small pony. So, again, p. 160, 'I'll lead you by your *Jack-a-lent hair*,' the 'Jack-a-lent' being a stuffed puppet, dressed in rags, *i.e.* a thing 'made up of patches, parings, shreds' (*Tale of a Tub*, iv. 2). Compare also *The Night Walker*, v. 1. vol. xi. p. 201: 'One has the *rug* and he's turned *Irish*'; *Satiromastix*, vol. i. p. 199, Pearson's Reprint, 'that Judas yonder that walks in *rug*'; *The Honest Whore*, vol. ii. p. 131, Pearson's Reprint, 'a *shag-haired cur*,' said of the Irish footman; *Richard III.*, ii. 1. 156, '*rug*-headed kerns'; *Macbeth*, iii. 1. 96, 'water-*rugs*,' *i.e.* rough-haired dogs.

Dyce's quotation is only another instance of the same misprint; for the 'leaden heeles' were the watch in their 'rug gowns,' coats of Irish frieze, their ordinary dress; cp. *e.g.* stage direction to *Lady Alimony*, iii. 5, Dodsley's Old Plays, vol. xiv. p. 332: 'Enter Constable and Watch, in *rug gowns*, bills, and dark lanthorns'; and note that the name of one of the Watch is 'Rugweed,' where *weed* = dress. Cp. also *A Woman Never Vexed*, ii. 1, Dodsley's

Old Plays, vol. xii. p. 127 : 'Thoud'st been press'd to death under two *Irish rugs*'; and *The Misfortunes of Arthur*, Argument to the second Act, Dodsley's Old Plays, vol. iv. p. 279 : 'There came a man bareheaded, *with long black shagged hair down to his shoulders, apparelled with an Irish jacket and shirt.*'

The Coxcomb, iv. 2. vol. iii. p. 181 :—

'I hate drink, there's the end on't,
And that man that drinks with meat is damn'd.'

For the metre's sake Sympson would read *without* instead of *with*, an alteration which, as Mason remarks, is no remedy. I propose,

'And *hold* that man that drinks with meat is damn'd.'

Wit at Several Weapons, i. 2. vol. iv. p. 16 :—

'*Witty.* Pax, there's nothing puts me besides my wits, but this fourth, this lay illiterate share ; there's no conscience in't.

. . . . .

Sir Ruin. Sir, be compendious ; either take or refuse : I will bate no token of my wife's share ; make even the last reckonings, and either so unite, or here divide company.

Pris. A good resolution *profecto* : let every man beg his own way, and happy man be his dole !

Witty. Well, here's your double share, and single brains ; *pol, ædepol,* here's toward a *castor ecastor* for you.'

On the words 'here's toward a *castor ecastor* for you,' Dyce notes, ' A friend observes to me, " *castor* (or *caster*,—and so the first folio spells the word) meant, in the canting language of rogues and vagabonds, a cloak; and hence the present pun." I doubt this explanation, though some quibble is evidently intended here.'

I find a totally different meaning in the words. Sir Ruinous Gentry, Wittypate, and Priscian have entered into a conspiracy for cheating people, and the scene opens with a dispute between Sir Ruinous and Wittypate as to whether a share of the proceeds is to be allowed to the former's wife for her help in the business. In the speech to which Dyce's note refers, Wittypate, imitating Priscian's scraps of Latinity, makes use of the oaths *pol*, *ædepol*, so frequent in Plautus and Terence. The mention of Pollux naturally suggests Castor and the equally frequent and correlative oath, *ecastor*. Reduplicating the word as *castor ecastor*, Wittypate again tenders money to Sir Ruinous. His meaning, then, is, 'here is something towards the double share you claim,' 'a *castor ecastor*' being equal to 'a reduplication, a double portion.'

Wit Without Money, i. 1. vol. iv. p. 111:—

"'Tis like enough; but pray satisfy me,
Are not these ways as honest as persecuting
The starv'd inheritance with musty corn
The very rats were fain to run away from, . . .

. . . .
. . . .

Do not I know your way of feeding beasts
With grains and windy stuff, to blow up butchers?
Your racking pastures, that have eaten up

Conjectural Readings 51

As many singing shepherds and their issues
As Andaluzia breeds? These are authentic.
I tell you, sir, I would not change ways with you,
Unless it were to sell your state that hour,
And, if it were possible, to spend it then too,
For all your *beans in Rumnillo.*'

Dyce notes, 'So all the old eds. Seward printed, "for all your *beasts* in *Rumney*"!! observing, "The uncle is before described as a great grazier; his beasts therefore are more likely to be mentioned as the chief of his wealth than his beans. Rumney Marsh in Kent is remarkably famous for fatting cattle; I think, therefore, my conjecture was probably *the true reading.*" The editors of 1778 adopted Seward's alteration. Weber left the old text undisturbed, remarking, "*Rumnillo* might, however, have been a cant *termination* for the same name [Rumney], or perhaps an arbitrary denomination for the uncle's estate." Qy. is the true reading, "For all your *benes* in *Rome-vile*"? *i.e.* for all your goods in London: in canting language *bene* is "good" and *Rome-vile* "London." . . .'

In spite of Dyce's scorn, I believe that Seward was not far wide of the mark; my suggestion is,

'For all your *beeves on Bromhille.*'

Bromhille being a hill on the outskirts of Romney Marsh: *your* may be taken generically. In the MS. of *The Faithful Friends*, i. 2. vol. iv. p. 214 'Bunhill' is spelt 'Bunnill,' the same mistake of *n* for *h*.

Wit Without Money, ii. 2. vol. iv. p. 119:—

> 'If you'll needs
> Do things of danger, do but lose yourselves,
> (Not any part concerns your understandings,
> For then you are meacocks, fools, and miserable);
> March off amain, within an inch of a *furcug*,
> Turn me o' the toe like a weathercock,
> Kill every day a sergeant for a twelvemonth,
> Rob the Exchequer, and burn all the rolls,
> And these will make a show.'

For *furcug* Theobald proposed *firelock*, and Weber printed *firecock*, a term, he says, by which the cock of a gun *may have been* denominated. Now, independent of the fact that *firecock*, in such a sense, does not exist, and that it is highly improbable Fletcher would have written *meacock*, *firecock*, *weathercock*, in three successive lines, *firelock* and *firecock* are equally out of place here. For it would be no greater proof of hardihood to 'turn o' the toe like a weathercock within an inch of' a firearm, than to stand up or do anything else in such a neighbourhood. The idea here is clearly parallel to that in *Lear*, v. 6. 24-26 :—

> 'You are now within a foot
> Of the extreme verge: for all beneath the moon
> Would I not leap upright':

and we want some synonym for *precipice*, *abyss*, to 'turn o' the toe like a weathercock within an inch of,' which would be to 'do a thing of danger.' I believe that we have here an image very frequent in Fletcher, and that for *furcug* we should read *Curtius-gulf*. In *The Custom of the Country*, iv. 4. vol. iv. p. 467, we have :—

> 'But women, women ! oh, the devil ! women !
> *Curtius's gulf* was never half so dangerous.'

In *The Double Marriage*, iv. 4. vol. vi. p. 393 :—

> 'Like *Curtius*
> I'll leap the *gulf* before you, fearless leap it.'

In *The Woman's Prize*, i. 2. vol. vii. p. 107 :—

> 'Like *Curtius*, to redeem my country, I have leap'd
> Into this *gulf* of marriage.'

In *The Bloody Brother*, iii. 1. vol. x. p. 424 :—

> 'The *Curtian gulf* of this conspiracy.'

As in the third of these passages, marriage is the danger that has been encountered, so in the passage before us marriage is the danger which Valentine is warning Harebrain and his fellows to avoid, the dangers he enumerates being preferable to it; and again in *The Custom of the Country* the danger is that which proceeds from women. For the form *Curtius-gulf*, compare *Bonduca*, ii. 1. vol. v. p. 27, 'this *Britain-gulf*'; also note that the second quarto and the folio spell *furcug* with a capital letter.

Wit Without Money, ii. 2. vol. iv. p. 121 :—

> 'Take a maid,
> A maid not worth a penny ; make her yours,
> Knead her, and mould her yours ; a maid worth nothing ;
> There is a virtuous spell in that word "nothing" ;

> A maid makes conscience
> Of half-a-crown a week for pins and puppets;
> A maid's content with one coach and two horses.'

'The first 4to,' says Dyce, 'has "a maid content";' and the first 4to is quite right, there being an ellipsis of *who* in the line 'A maid makes conscience.'

Wit Without Money, iii. 1. vol. iv. p. 139:—
> 'May zealous smiths
> So housel all our hackneys that they may feel
> Compunction in their feet, and tire at Highgate.'

Seward and Dyce are no doubt right, in spite of Weber's conjecture, in taking *housel* as a profane allusion to the Eucharist; but they have not noticed that in 'comp*unction*' there is a further allusion to the rite of extreme *unction*.

Wit Without Money, iii. 1. vol. iv. p. 139:—
> '*Hum.* At St. Albans, let all the inns be drunk,
> Not an host sober, to bid her worship welcome!
> *Short.* Not a fiddle, but all preach'd down by puritans;
> No meat but legs of beef!
> *Hum.* No beds but woolpacks!
> *Short.* And those so cramm'd
> With warrens of starv'd fleas that bite like ban-dogs.
> Let Mims be angry at their St. bel-swagger,
> And we pass in the heat on't, and be beaten,
> Beaten abominably, beaten horse and man,
> And all my lady's linen sprinkled
> With suds and dish-water.'

'" Mims is in the neighbourhood of St. Albans, and some local custom, tumultuously celebrated, is plainly alluded to in this speech. It was, we doubt not, familiarly known in the times of our authors; but we have in vain endeavoured to trace its memory or discover its origin."—Ed. 1778. The allusion here is as dark to me as to the other editors' . . . (Dyce), who quotes from Richardson's *Dictionary*, ' Bel-swagger. Perhaps no more than a fine, a brave, *swaggerer*, a braggart, a bully,' and the passage cited there and by Johnson from Dryden's *Spanish Friar*, act v., in which the term is used in such sense. Murray, *English Dictionary*, gives other instances with the same meaning. As to this convenient 'local custom,' I am very sceptical, and believe that the line here indicates nothing more than the anger of Mims at the drunken revelry of its swaggering neighbour with its aristocratic prefix of ' St.,' anger which it vents upon all coming from that place.

Wit Without Money, iii. 1. vol. iv. p. 142 :—
> ' In you men
> 'Tis held a coolness, if you lose your right,
> Affronts and loss of honour.'

Punctuate,
> 'if you lose your right
> Affronts, and loss of honour.'

i.e. it is considered as a slight and loss of honour if you do not receive the salutations due to your rank.

Wit Without Money, iv. 2. vol. iv. p. 159 :—
> ' But, Luce, didst ever know a woman melt so?
> She is finely hurt to *hunt*.'

What does *hunt* mean here? Qy. *heart*? So in *The Knight of Malta*, ii. 1. vol. v. p. 128, the folios give *hurt* for *heart*.

Wit Without Money, iv. 4. vol. iv. p. 172:—

'Do you think you are here, sir,
  Amongst your waistcoateers, your base wenches
  That *scratch* at such occasions?'

Qy. *snatch*? Possibly the scribe taking the words 'the woman will not *bite*,' a few lines above, in a literal sense, thought that *scratch* was a continuation of the idea.

Wit Without Money, iv. 5. vol. iv. p. 176:—

'You shall stay till I talk with you,
And not dine neither, but fastingly my fury;
You think you have undone me; think so still
. . . . .
Till you return to what I found ye, people
Betrayed into the hands of fencers', challengers',
Tooth-drawers' bills, and tedious proclamations
In meal markets, with throngings to see cut-purses;
(Stir not, but hear and mark; I'll cut your throats else)—
Till water-works, and rumours of New Rivers,
Rid you again, and run you into questions
Who built *the Thames*.'

Dyce notes, 'The first 4to has "built *Theamea*"; the second 4to and the folio read "built *Thames*." "The allusion to the New River, projected in the time of James I., is sufficiently plain. That to the *building of the Thames* is not explicable as sense; but the authors most probably wish only to exemplify the absurd stupidity of the conversation among the three suitors, previous to their acquaintance with Valentine."— WEBER. If *built the Thames* be the right reading (which I greatly doubt), it may perhaps mean—built bridges over the Thames.'

Now, I must premise that in no single play of our authors are there so many corruptions of the text as in the present one. The printer of the first quarto was evidently not only a very careless but a very ignorant man, and when he came to proper names, was greatly at a loss. I must also, before coming to my conjecture, notice the word *water-works*, which is important to the understanding of the passage. The reference is to a particular water-work described in Stowe's *Survey of London*, p. 294, quoted by Nares: 'Within the gate of this house [Bigod's house] (now belonging to the citie of London), is lately, to wit, in the yeare 1594 and 1595, builded one large house of great height, called an engine, made by Bevis Bulmar, gentleman, for conveying and forcing of Thames water to serve in the middle and west parts of the cities.' To this water-work Jonson in his *Alchemist*, a play first acted in 1610, refers, ii. 1. p. 47, ed. Gifford: 'As he that built *the water-work* does with the water'; and again iii. 2. p. 105: 'being cessed at eighteen pence, for *the water-work*.' It was evidently, therefore, a work of great importance. Of a similar nature, though on a larger scale, was the New River, the opening of which was celebrated by a public pageant on Michaelmas Day, 1613 (the dramatist Middleton writing the speech), and which would be fresh in the memory of those who saw *Wit Without Money*, produced soon after 1614, for the first time. Weber's supposition that 'our authors probably wish only to exemplify the absurd stupidity of the conversation among the three suitors previous to their acquaintance with Valentine,' seems to me a most extravagant one. Though Valentine constantly taunts them with their stupidity, or rather their ignorance of the world, he throughout addresses them as men to be reasoned with, and also mentions their having been at the University. On the other hand, if 'built Thames,' or 'built the Thames,' can mean 'built bridges over the Thames,' then, it seems to me that anything can mean anything. My belief is that we should read 'who built the *Aniena*.' The *Aniena* (Aqua) was the greatest of the aqueducts of Rome, being to that city what Bulmar's water-work and the New River were to London. It extended some sixty miles in length, and over the double arch which spanned it and the Claudia, there were three inscriptions which recorded the names of Claudius as the builder, and of Vespasian and Titus as the restorers, of the aqueduct. The suitors, though University men, may not have known anything of this aqueduct, but Fletcher no doubt did, and he is by no means careful to adapt the language of his characters to the understanding of the speakers or of those addressed. If the words *Theamea* and *The aniena* be compared stroke for stroke, it will be found that but for the omission of the one letter *n* in the final syllable, they are absolutely identical; and it is a curious fact that in this play the letter *n* is frequently omitted, its place being supplied by a horizontal stroke over the vowel immediately preceding, a stroke which might easily have been omitted here. It will, perhaps, be objected to my conjecture that no compositor, however careless, would print the article with a capital, and the proper name with a small letter. To this I answer that twice in Dekker's *Honest Whore*, vol. ii. p. 32, Pearson's Reprint, 'the Antelope,' the name of a tavern, is printed 'Th' antilop'; and so again, without any mark of elision, in Chapman's *Blind Beggar of Alexandria*, vol. i. p. 45, Pearson's Reprint, we have, ' Men say, my lord, he cast his desperate body From *Thalexandrian* tower into the sea.' Add Sir Thomas Wyatt's *Complaint upon Love*, l. 88, 'And *Thaffricaine* Scipion the famous.' Here the corruption into *Thames* would be made all the easier by the fact of the water for the water-work being supplied from that river. I take the meaning of the sentence to be ' till your ears are so dinned with talk about water-works and New Rivers, that you begin to speculate about the builders of the Anienan aqueduct.'

Wit Without Money, v. 2. vol. iv. p. 184 :—
  'Take his *Nellson*.'

So, says Dyce 'the first 4to, the second 4to, and the folio have, "Take *this* Nelson"; and so Seward who pointed the words thus, "Take this, Nelson." Weber says that *Nellson* is " probably a cant term for a sword "; rather, I believe, for a club.'

Read 'his *keelson*.' The *keelson*, or *kelson*, is the beam that battens down the flooring of the lowest deck to the keel; and the cudgel with which Lance is ready to 'labour,' *i.e.* belabour, his master is humorously likened to this beam. Note that Valentine has already likened Lance to a ship of war named after the Dutch admiral, Peter Bassel, and used the nautical metaphor 'bear up' (curiously enough the same phrase as that used by Stephano in *Tempest*, iii. 2. 3, to his fellow drunkards, '*bear up*, and board 'em '); also that in calling Lance 'Peter Bassel' he alludes to his Dutch courage inspired by 'sack.' Cotgrave gives, ' *Quille*. The keel of a ship; also a keyl, a big peg, or pin of wood, used at nine-pins or keyls, etc.'

The Faithful Friends, i. 1. vol. iv. p. 200 :—
  'Do you, then, malign his happiness. . . .?'

The MS. has, 'Do you then malign *then* his happiness . . .?'

Read,
> 'Do you malign, then, *this* his happiness. . . . ?'

The omission of *this* before *his* is not uncommon.

The Faithful Friends, i. 1. vol. iv. p. 204 :—

> '*Learch.* Tullius is general, and with greatest pomp
> Is coming this way; the king leaning thus
> Upon his shoulder; eyeing as they pass
> The looks and gestures of each gazer-on,
> How they relish his election.
> *Ruf.* But rawly without salt;
> They have a fresh soldier to their general.'

Surely a full stop should be put after 'gazer-on,' and the next line, with the reading, 'How relish they his election?' be given to Rufinus, Learchus answering, 'But rawly,' etc. Both sense and metre seem to demand this.

The Faithful Friends, iv. 1. vol. iv. p. 273 :—

> 'Villain, keep off!
> Thou art *mad*, a pandar, nay, what's worse,
> A traitor to thy friend.'

Dyce remarks, 'There seems to be some corruption here.' I feel sure we should read 'thou art *made* a pandar,' *i.e.* you have become a pandar. Tullius is under the impression that Armanus had been a party to the plot for seducing his wife, Philadelpha.

The Widow, i. 2. vol. iv. p. 318 :—

> '*Ric.* Say you so, sir?
> I'll try your ladyship's faith.—Lady, well met.

> *Franc.* I do not think so.
> *Ric.* A scornful *gom*? and at the first dash too!
> My widow never gave me such an answer.'

'" Junius in his etymologicon says that *gom* or *gome* signifies a man. Ricardo therefore means that Francisco, in his assumed character of a woman, acts not with the softness and delicacy of a female, but with the scorn and haughtiness of a male."—REED. Surely "*gom*" (though the present passage is quoted under that word, both by Todd and Nares) cannot be the right reading. Qy. "glum"? *i.e.* a gloomy, sour look.' (Dyce.)

Read *gum*, *i.e.* flout, piece of insolence.

The Widow, v. 1. vol. iv. p. 381:—

> 'Hang thyself when thou wilt, a slave *go* with thee!'

Read, 'a slave *goes* with thee!'

Bonduca, i. 1. vol. v. p. 7:—

> 'Are these the men that conquer by inheritance?
> The fortune-makers? these the Julians
> That with the sun measure the end of nature,
> Making the world but one Rome and one Cæsar?
> Shame how they flee! *Cæsar's* soft soul dwells in 'em;
> Their mothers got 'em sleeping, Pleasure nursed 'em.'

Read, '*Ease's* soft soul dwells in 'em,' corresponding with 'Pleasure nurs'd 'em,' *Cæsar's* being caught from the line above. In *Valentinian*, v. 8 'please her' rhymes with 'Cæsar.'

The Knight of Malta, ii. 2. vol. v. p. 134:—

> 'I have seen him scale
> As if a falcon had run up a train,

Clashing his warlike pinions, his steel'd cuirass,
And at his pitch *inmew* the town below him.'

Read *ennew*, and see note, p. 150, on Heywood's *Woman Kill'd with Kindness*. The words *pinions*, *pitch*, etc., are, as Weber says, used metaphorically: but the verb does not here mean to 'inclose in a mew or cage,' as he adds. A falcon is *inmewed* or *enmewed* while it is moulting, but does not itself *inmew* or *enmew* anything.

The Knight of Malta, iii. 4. vol. v. p. 167 :—

' No entertainment's perfect
Without it, on my word, no livery like it ;
I'll tell her he looks for it as duly
As for his fee ; there's no suit got without it ;
Gold is an ass to 't.'

Mason conjectures,

' *Your lawyer*, he looks,' etc.

I would rather retain the words, *I'll tell her* and read,

' *I'll tell her the lawyer* looks,' etc.

The change is less, merely the insertion of *lawyer*, and the metre is improved.

The Knight of Malta, iv. 2. vol. v. p. 186 :—

'Thou art a dog, I'll make thee swear, a dog *stav'd*,
A mangy cur-dog.'

Weber explains *stav'd* as 'beaten with staves'; Heath as 'beaten from his hold.' Qy. *starv'd*?

Valentinian, iv. 4. vol. v. p. 287 :—

> 'Thou canst fight well, and bravely,
> Thou canst endure all dangers, heats, colds, hungers;
> Heaven's angry flashes are not suddener
> Than I have seen thee execute, nor more mortal;
> The wingèd feet of flying enemies
> I have stood and view'd thee mow away like rushes,
> And *still kill the killer* : were thy mind
> But half so sweet in peace,' etc.

Though no commentator has noticed the italicised words, their want of meaning, their cacophony, and the imperfection of the metre, show, I think, that the line is corrupt. I would read,

> 'And still *toil* kill the killer':

i.e. though you mowed them down like rushes, so great was their number that you were almost dead with the mere labour of slaying. The word *toil* is sufficiently like *kill* to have been accidentally omitted. Cf. *Bonduca*, i. 2. vol. v. p. 22,

> 'They [the enemy] are so infinite, so ever-springing,
> We shall be kill'd with killing' :

ii. 1. p. 27,

> 'Where we lie buried quick above the ground,
> And are, with labouring sweat and breathless pain,
> *Kill'd* like to slaves, and cannot *kill* again!'

and *A Wife for a Month*, v. 3. vol. ix. p. 382, 'But what . . . *kill'd with killing.*'

The Laws of Candy, iii. 3. vol. v. p. 364 :—

> 'Alas, it is a misery I grieve
> To put you to! and I will suffer rather
> *In his* tyranny, than thou in mine.'

Altered by Seward to '*under* his tyranny':
Qy. 'In *this* his tyranny'?

The Queen of Corinth, i. 2. vol. v. p. 404 :—

> 'If I speak
> Too much, *though I confess I speak well*,
> Prithee remember 'tis a woman's weakness,
> And then thou wilt forgive it.'

Sympson would insert *not* after *confess*; Seward, *not* after *I*. Qy. 'though I confess *not*, I speak *ill*'? One does not confess that one speaks *well* —except to one's-self. My alteration completes the metre of the line.

The Queen of Corinth, iii. 1. vol. v. p. 440 :—

> 'And whate'er he be
> Can with unthankfulness *assoil* me, let him
> Dig out mine eyes, and sing my name in verse,
> In ballad verse,' etc.

Surely *assail*.

The Loyal Subject, iv. 3. vol. vi. p. 85 :—

> 'Words steep'd in honey,
> That will so melt into your minds, *buy* chastity
> A thousand ways, a thousand knots to tie ye.'

Qy. *ply*? *buy* can hardly be right.

The Loyal Subject, iv. 4. vol. vi. p. 88 :—

> 'A dog! drunken people,
> That in their pot see visions, and turn *states*
> Madmen and children!'

Seward printed *statists*: possibly *statesmen*, the

suffix being omitted owing to the proximity of 'madmen.' Compare *Coriolanus*, i. 1. 180-186.

The Mad Lover, Epilogue, l. 2. vol. vi. p. 212:—

> 'Here lies the doubt now; let our plays be good,
> Our own *care* sailing equal in the flood,
> Our preparations new, new our attire,
> Yet we are here becalm'd still, in the mire,
> Here we stick fast. Is there no way to clear
> The passage of our judgment, and our fear?'

For *care*, I would read *crare*, *i.e.* boat. This seems to be shown by 'becalm'd,' 'stick fast,' and 'passage.' The word occurs in *The Captain*, i. 2. vol. iii. p. 230, 'Let him venture in some decay'd *crare* of his own,' where it has a figurative sense.

The False One, ii. 2. vol. vi. p. 250:—

> 'Now I will outbrave all, make all my servants [drunk],
> And my brave deed shall be writ in wine for virtuous.'

Here *drunk* is an insertion of Dyce's which was questioned by a correspondent, T. S., and defended by Dyce in his *Addenda et Corrigenda*.

I think T. S. is certainly right. Though Septimius is afterwards seen in 'brave apparel,' what he boasts here is that he will no longer shrink before those who scorn him, but will meet them with a brave face now that he has gold to back him up; while 'make all my servants' is merely a hyperbolical expression. Of his servants we nowhere hear anything; but in a later scene, iii. 2, he has the audacity to patronise Antony, Dolabella, and Scæva with offers of money and wine, and immediately afterwards tries to 'make' their disabled soldiers his 'servants,' employing the same temptation of wine. In the latter of the two lines I am inclined to think that *brave* has been caught from the former.

The False One, iv. 3. vol. vi. p. 289:—

'*Sept.* Womanish fear, farewell! I'll never melt more :—
Lead on to some great thing, to *wake* my spirit :
I cut the cedar Pompey, and I'll fell
This huge oak Cæsar too.
Pho.   Now thou sing'st sweetly,
And Ptolemy shall crown thee for thy service·
Achil. He's well wrought ; put him apace for cooling.'

Wake is the reading of the second folio, adopted by all modern editors, though Dyce conjectures *steel*. The first folio gives *weale*, and this I believe to be perfectly sound, it being nothing else than an older spelling of the modern *weld*. The earliest form of the word, *wel* (later *welle*), was in use at all events as late as 1570. It comes from the Anglo-Saxon *weallan*, to boil, and the present *d* is a late excrescence. Here to *weld* agrees better than *wake* or *steel* with the context *melt, wrought*, and *cooling*. It is also in keeping with *cut* and *fell*.

The Double Marriage, v. 3. vol. vi. p. 409 :—

'We are cold,
Cold walls shall not keep him from us.'

Read '*Stone* walls'; *Cold* being caught from the previous line.

The Humorous Lieutenant, iii. 5. vol. vi. p. 478 :—

'What a *flatten* face he has now!'

The MS. gives *slotten*. I would read *shotten*; Compare *Women Pleased*, ii. 4. 9, 'My *shotten* friend'; *Wit Without Money*, ii. 4. 2, 'You *shotten-*soul'd slight fellows.'

Women Pleased, iv. 1. vol. vii. p. 57 :—

'The people simple, plain, and harmless-witty,
Whose honest labours Heaven rewards with plenty
Of corn, wine, oil, *which they again as thankful*,
To their new crops new pastimes celebrate,
And crown their joyful harvests with new voices.'

Heath and Dyce think that something has fallen out here, and pronounce the passage as it stands to be nonsense. If any alteration were necessary, *while* for *which* would make the sense quite clear, viz., while they on their part, in return, express their gratitude by new pastimes in honour of their new crops, etc. But *which* was often used of old adverbially = as to which.

The Woman's Prize, ii. 4. vol. vii. p. 139 :—

'She should *ride the wild mare* once a week, she should,
Believe me, friends, she should; I would tabor her.'

Dyce says that Petruchio means 'that his wife should be mounted on something, and well drubbed.' The 'something' is surely the 'cucking-stool,' a common engine for the punishment of shrews and scolds, while in 'I would tabor her,' *i.e.* make her dance with a cudgel, there is perhaps an allusion to Katharina's vigorous treatment of Hortensio in *The Taming of the Shrew*, ii. 1. 157, when he 'stood amazed for a while, As on a pillory, looking through the hole.'

The Woman's Prize, ii. 4. vol. vii. p. 140 :—

> 'They heave ye stool on stool, and fling main pot-lids
> Like massy rocks, dart ladles, tossing irons,
> And tongs like thunderbolts.'

Sympson proposed '*toasting* irons'; Nares thinks 'tossing irons' means pokers; rather, I fancy, shovels.

The Woman's Prize, ii. 6. vol. vii. p. 144 :—

> 'I peep'd in
> At a loose *lansket*.'

It has been conjectured that *lansket* means the panel of a door, or a lattice, or a lancet-window. The last of these seemed negatived by the word 'loose.' I believe we should read *wainscot*, of old spelt *wainskot*, and used not merely for the wainscot against a wall, but for partitions, etc. In *The Elder Brother*, iv. 4. vol. x. p. 270, we have, 'He had better have stood between two *panes of wainscot*'; though there the phrase is used figuratively of the pillory. Cp. also *The Fair Maid of the Inn*, v. 2. vol. x. p. 92, 'I saw him this morning, through a chink of *wainscot* that divides my lodging and the Host's of the house.'

Monsieur Thomas, ii. 3. vol. vii. p. 338 :—

> 'He ne'er *perceives* 'em
> Longer than looking on.'

Qy. '*pursues*'? Sam refers to the fickleness of Hylas.

Monsieur Thomas, iii. 1. vol. vii. p. 349 :—

> 'Equal affections [*born*] and shot together.'

The word *born* was 'inserted,' says Dyce, 'by the editors of 1778. Both in the 4to and in the folio the line stands thus :—

> "Equal affections   and shot together."

'Seward printed,

> "Equal affections, and shot *up* together."'

The metaphor does not seem to me from plants but from arrows both levelled and discharged together. I would therefore read,

> 'Equal affections, *aim'd* and shot together.'

From its resemblance to *and*, *aim'd* might easily have been dropped by the transcriber.

The Island Princess, iii. 1. vol. vii. p. 458 :—

> '*Ruy.* My private benefits I have forgot, sir;
> But those you might lay claim to as my follower,
> Yet some men would remember;—
> *Pin.* I do daily.
> *Ruy.* The place which I have put you in, which is no
>   weak one;
> Next to myself you stand in all employments,' etc.

'Heath's explanation of this passage (which agrees with Mason's) is,' says Dyce, 'as follows: "I have forgot, and think not worth urging, the benefits I have conferred on you in my private character as a friend and near relation; but yet there are men who would remember those benefits which, as one of my followers and in common with the rest of them, you might think yourself entitled to a share of, and with which I have distinguished you above the others," etc. Weber gives a different, and, I think, an erroneous interpretation.'

Heath's explanation seems to me to slur over *but* and *yet*. I would punctuate thus:—

> 'My private benefits I have forgot, sir,—
> But those you might lay claim to as my followers,—
> Yet some men,' etc.

with the explanation, 'I have forgotten the private benefits I have conferred on you—but (*those I need not refer to, for*) you might lay claim to them as my follower—yet some men,' etc. Such ellipses are very frequent.

The Pilgrim, ii. 2. vol. viii. p. 30:—

> 'Then thou should'st have brav'd me,
> And, arm'd with all thy family's hate, upon me
> Done something *worthy feat.*'

Sympson put a comma after *something*; Weber a hyphen to connect *something* and *worthy*, i.e. worthy in some degree, a sense which Dyce rightly says the words could not bear unless preceded by the article *a*. Seward conjectured, '*Have* done *some* worthy feat'; Mitford, 'Done *some* feat worthy *thee*.'

I believe we should read, 'Done something *worth thy* feat.'

The Wild-Goose Chase, i. 1. vol. viii. p. 117 :—

> 'Within this eight hours I took leave of him,
> And over-*hied* him, having some slight business
> That forc'd me out o' the way.'

'Both the old eds. "over-*ey'd*,"' says Dyce; 'and so Sympson, though he pronounced it to be a corruption, and proposed "over-*rid*," and "over-*yed*." The editors of 1778 printed "over-*rid*," and conjectured "over-*hied*," which was adopted by Weber, and which certainly seems to be the right reading.'

I would read 'over-*vy'd*' (the old spelling of *vied*), *i.e.* out-vied him in my speed. There were formerly many compounds of to *vie* (used at games of cards), *e.g. out-vie, re-vie*, and probably *over-vie* was among them.

The Wild-Goose Chase, iv. 1. vol. viii. p. 176 :—

> 'One of your London light-o-loves, a right one,
> Came over in thin pumps and half a petticoat,
> One *faith*, and one smock, with a broken haberdasher.'

'"The word *faith* seems a corruption here." Ed. 1778. "The text seems to imply possessing just as much faith and as large a stock of linen as a bankrupt haberdasher whose credit is destroyed and his goods seized by law."—Weber' (Dyce).

Weber's explanation is simply ridiculous. Read, 'One *fall*,' *i.e.* falling-band. Compare Middleton, *Your Five Gallants*, i. 1. 81, 'A fine white beaver band, three *falls*; I ha' known her have more in her days'; *Michaelmas Term*, i. 2. 16, 'wires and tires . . . felts and *falls*.' Ladies of this class seem to have been particular in the matter of this article of dress; compare Dekker, *The Honest Whore*, vol. ii. p. 41, Pearson's Reprint, 'I would thou wouldst give me five yards of lawn to make my punk some *falling bands* o' the fashion, three falling upon one another; for that's the new edition now.'

The Sea-Voyage, i. 2. vol. viii. p. 302 :—

> '*Where* a mighty storm sever'd our barks, that *where*
> My wife, my daughter, and my noble ladies
> That went with her, virgins and loving souls,
> To scape those pirates—'

'At Seward's suggestion,' says Dyce, 'Sympson omitted this word [*where*], and made some alterations in the next two speeches. There is some gross corruption here. Qy. should the second *where* be *bore*?'

Against Dyce's suggestion it may be urged that *bore* is rather a violent change for *where*, that *that*, referring to *barks*, will have to be taken as=one of which bore (for, as is seen from v. 4. p. 367, there were but two barks, 'the one bore all the able men ... in the other the women were embarked'), and that *bore* will not, in point of construction, go well with the broken sentence, 'To scape those pirates ——.' Further, it seems to me that both rhythm and sense indicate corruption in the former *where*. I would therefore read,

'*Whereon* a mighty storm sever'd our barks, that *there*,' etc.

i.e. so that there (in that storm) my wife, etc., in order to escape those pirates, etc.

The Spanish Curate, v. 2. vol. viii. p. 481 :—

'They have played their prizes with me,
And with their several flurts have lighted dangerously.'

Seward reads '*they've* lighted *danger*.' The editors of 1778 supposed *lighted* to mean 'trifled,' though they produce no authority for such a meaning. Mason explains, 'they had succeeded in their several flurts, and that to his prejudice'; comparing, for the neuter sense of *lighted*, *Macbeth*, ii. 3. 148, 'This murderous shaft that's shot Hath not yet *lighted*.' Dyce explains, 'They have ... with me' as 'they have played their feats, pranks.' But neither Mason nor Dyce seems to me to bring out the full sense of the passage, which I take to be this: 'They have ventured to cross swords with me (as pupils in fencing did with the master when being tested for their certificates as scholars, "playing their prizes" as it was called) in order to prove how cunning of fence they are, and their various passes of wit have come dangerously near wounding my reputation.'

Beggars' Bush, iii. 4. vol. ix. p. 67 :—
> 'Now for *myself*.'

Read, 'my *help*,' *i.e.* the help promised him by Clause. Heath would read '*his help*,' with the same meaning.

Beggars' Bush, v. 2. vol. ix. p. 103 :—
> 'The spirit of Bottom is grown bottomless.'

Of this allusion to *Midsummer Night's Dream* Steevens says: 'It may mean that either the public grew indifferent to bad actors, to plays in general, or to actors the humour of which consisted in blunders.' On which Dyce remarks: 'Whatever be the meaning of the passage, I do not believe that Steevens has hit it by any of his conjectures.'

Certainly not. I once thought the meaning was, 'The spirit of Bottom which was equal to any undertaking, equal to playing any part, however ambitious, has had its bottom knocked out,' *i.e.* we, without our former allies, can no longer undertake such exploits as of old, but must content ourselves with mere petty filching. But perhaps we might read, 'The spirit of Bottom's *not* grown bottomless.' Higgen (the speaker) has just said,

> 'Higgen will seek
> *Some safer shelter*, in some other climate
> *With this his tatter'd colony* :'

and, as spokesman of the Beggars, 'orator Higgen,' 'the fine well-spoken Higgen,' is not without resemblance to Bottom.

A Wife for a Month, i. 4. vol. ix. p. 326 :—

'Those are poor fools,
A set, people call them honest.'

'The folios,' says Dyce, 'have no comma after *set*. Seward proposed to read, "*Yet* people call them honest," and Sympson, "*And yet* people," etc. The editors of 1778 supposed that "A set people" might perhaps signify, formal, precise people. Heath (*M.S. Notes*) conjectured "A set *of* people," etc. Mason first gave the right punctuation, comparing what Sorano says (act v. sc. 3) :—

"They are such
The foolish call their country's honour,"' etc.

I think we should punctuate,

'A set, people call them, honest.'

i.e. an honest set, at least so people call them.

Rule a Wife and Have a Wife, i. 2. vol. ix. p. 403 :—

'To be tied to a man's pleasure is a second labour.'

'To obtain a man's pleasure,' says Mason, 'is the first labour; to be tied to it, a second. This appears to be Sanchio's meaning.' Does it not rather mean that compulsion to pleasure is only another name for labour?

The Fair Maid of the Inn, ii. 2. vol x. p. 36:—

> 'I'll tend my master, and instantly be with you for a cup of *cherelly*.'

So the first folio; the second gives *cherally*. No other instance has been found of either form. Murray, *English Dictionary*, suggests an analogy with *bonally*; but *bonally* is not the *name* of a liquor, nor does to 'drink *bonally*' mean more than to 'drink *bon voyage*.' Possibly we should read *cheerbelly*, *i.e. belly-cheer*. That word, though generally used of food, would equally apply to 'wine that maketh glad the heart of man'; and it is a clown who is speaking.

The Fair Maid of the Inn, iii. 1. vol. x. p. 49:—

> 'My often visits, sweet Bianca, cannot
> But constantly inform thy judgment wherein
> *Thy* happiness consists.'

Qy. *My*?

The Fair Maid of the Inn, iii. 2. vol. x. p. 53:—

> 'Though divided
> I stand between the laws of Truth and Modesty,
> Yet let my griefs have vent; *yet* the clearness
> Of strange necessity requires obedience
> To Nature and your mercy.'

Qy. *for*?

The Fair Maid of the Inn, iii. 2. vol. x. p. 53:—

> 'Wherein, if strict opinion *cancel* shame,
> My frailty is my plea.'

'The meaning of this sentence,' says Mason, 'appears to me to be this: If the strictness of my principles gets the better of my shame, and induces me to reveal what I should blush to confess, let my frailty plead my excuse.'

Qy. '*counsel* shame'? In Webster's *The Devil's Law Case*, p. 135/1, ed. Dyce, *where precisely the same incident occurs*, Leonora, when asked why she so late reveals the truth, answers :—

> 'Because, my lord, I loath'd that such a sin
> Should lie smother'd with me in my grave, my penitence
> Though to my shame, prefers the revealing of it
> 'Bove worldly reputation.'

The Noble Gentleman, i. 2. vol. x. p. 123 :—

> 'Think her fair
> And great, *clapt in* velvet,—she is so.'

'Sympson,' says Dyce, 'printed *yclad*, and so the editors of 1778! Heath (*MS. Notes*) would read "*clasped*." I believed that the poet wrote, "And great, *and* clapt," etc.'

Qy. 'clapt *up*?'

The Noble Gentleman, iii. 2. vol. x. p. 149 :—

> ''Twill be rarely strange
> To see him stated thus, as though he went
> A shroving through the city, or intended
> To set up some new *stake*.'

Sympson understands *stake* to mean a Maypole; Dyce takes it for a 'magnifico's post,' as in *The Fair Maid of the Inn*, iii. 1. Qy. *statue?*

The Noble Gentleman, v. 1. vol. x. p. 187:—

'*First Gent.* Monsieur Marine, pray, let me speak with you;
Sir, I must *wave* you to conceal this *party*;
It stands upon *my* utter overthrow.
Seem not discontented, nor do not stir a foot,
For if you do, you and your hope—
I swear you are a lost man, if you stir!'

'Sympson,' says Dyce '(after proposing a needless alteration of the passage), explained "*party*—resolution of going down,"' etc.

Mason would alter 'party' to '*parley*'; and Weber says, '" The Gentleman requests Marine to conceal the party or side which he took by giving him such advice," etc. I believe that 'this party' is used δεικτικῶς, and is equivalent to—me, the person addressing you. Heath, not understanding the passage, would read "*your*" [for *my*, l. 3].'

I suggest,

'Sir, I must *warn* you to conceal this *parting*,'

and perhaps, with Heath, *your* for *my*. The object of the First Gentleman is to befool both Marine and Clermont by persuading them to stay at court and fall in with the ways of those about it, so that he and his friends may make love to their wives. As he says, iv. 4. p. 175, 'To me the fooling of this fool is venery'; and when Clermont, p. 174, is angry at Longueville's familiarity with his wife, the Gentleman addresses him in almost the same words as he uses here:—

> 'Let her alone : be wise ; stir not a foot ;
> For, if you do, all your hopes are buried ;
> I swear you are a lost man if you stir.'

In Marine's case the Gentleman endeavours to detain him at court by pretending that the king is angry at the idea of his departing, and that he must do all in his power to hide the fact that he was already on the point of setting out. 'It stands upon *my* utter overthrow' may perhaps be nothing more than the Gentleman's exaggerated pretence that, if Marine goes, all the blame will be cast upon him ; but he is so strongly emphasising the ruin of Marine's hopes, that *your* looks more probable. *Parting=departing* is of course frequent enough.

The Elder Brother, iii. 1. vol. x. p. 235 :—

> 'He's young, and may be good, yet he must make it ;
> And I may help, and *help'd too, thank him also.*'

'Old eds.,' says Dyce,

> "He's young, and may be good, yet he must make it ;
> And I may helpe, and *helpe* to thank him also."

'Theobald printed :—

> He's young, and may be good, yet he must make *him so*,
> And I may help, and *for help* thank him also"——

the conjectural emendation of Seward, who observed: "The sense I take to be this: He's yet too young to be fixed to either good or evil, but he may hereafter make himself good, and I may help to make him so; and, as I am young, he, in return, may help to fix me in goodness. The slight reformation I have offered entirely gives this sense." I have adopted (with Weber) the much slighter alteration which was introduced into the text by the editors of 1778.'

Seward's explanation seems to me a very strained one. Angelina has shown no doubts about herself, no symptom of thinking that she needs to be 'fixed in goodness.' Perhaps we might read :—

'And I may help and *hope to win thanks also.*'

The Elder Brother, iii. 3. vol. x. p. 242 :—

'*Eust.* These are but harsh words, uncle.
Mir.   So I mean 'em.
Sir, you play harsher play wi' your elder brother.
Eust. I would be loath to *give* you.
Mir.   Do not venture ;
I'll make your wedding-clothes sit closer to you, then.

On the words, 'I would be loath to *give* you,' Dyce says, '*i.e. harsher play which* I would be loath to give you.'

I believe we should read, 'I would be loath to *grieve* you.'

F

The Elder Brother, v. 1. vol. x. p. 286 :—

> 'For your credit,
> Which you think you have lost, spare Charles, and swinge me,
> And soundly, three or four walking velvet cloaks,
> That wear no swords to guard 'em, yet deserve it,
> Thou art made up again.'

'Theobald, at Seward's suggestion, printed "that wear swords *not* to guard 'em." The editors of 1778, "That wear *not* swords to guard 'em." Seward reads *not* instead of *no*; because, as he says, Eustace could give no proof of his valour by beating three or four beaux, who had no swords to defend themselves with. But there is little force in this reasoning, as there is as much prowess in swinging [? swingeing] a man who had no sword by his side, as in beating one who dare not draw the sword he had. It appears to me that the old reading is the true one, and that it was the intention of the authors to reprobate in this place the fashion which then prevailed amongst the young gentlemen of going without swords, as they did in *The Custom of the Country*, when Duarte, finding Alonzo armed with a dagger only, insults him in the grossest manner and says :—

> "Such as you are
> Have studied the undoing of poor cutlers,
> And made all manly weapons out of fashion ;
> You carry poniards to murder men,
> Yet dare not wear *a sword to guard* your honour."

'To which Rutilio adds :—

> "That's true, indeed. Upon my life, this gallant
> Is brib'd to repeal *banish'd swords*."

'And Alonzo afterwards (vol. iv. p. 254) says,—

> "I am paid,
> For being in the fashion."—MASON (Dyce).'

Surely all is this very far-fetched. I agree, indeed, with Mason that the text is sound; but I put a very different interpretation upon the passage, *viz.* 'who although they do not, like Charles, go about with swords to guard them (and so give you the same opportunity of proving your valour), yet deserve beating for their silly vanity.' In Mason's explanation the adversative *yet* is overlooked, and with it we should have had *and*.

The Elder Brother, v. 2. vol. x. p. 289 :—

> 'In what is my *love* Charles defective, sir?'

The old editions, except the quarto of 1651, read *lord*, and so Theobald. Read *lov'd*, and compare Marston, *The Fawn*, v. 1. 213, where conversely the old editions read 'sole *lov'd*' instead of 'sole *lord*.'

The Nice Valour, ii. 1. vol. x. p. 305 :—

> 'You ha' not seen the like, madam ;
> A monster worth your sixpence, *lovely worth*.'

Qy. '*lively* worth '*t*,' *i.e.* thoroughly deserving it?

The Nice Valour, ii. 1. vol. x. p. 314 :—

'For I can cog with you—

. . . . .

Talk of battalions, woo you in a skirmish;
Divine my mind to you, lady; and, being sharp set,
Can court you at half-pike—or name your weapon,
We cannot fail you, lady.'

With Seward, who gives *discharge* (adopted by the editors of 1778, and approved by Mason), I believe that a technical term of war is here needed and I would read *darraign, i.e.* draw out in battle array. The word was of old spelt *darraine, darrayne, darreigne, darreine, derine*; and the last form is very near to *divine*. The word was moreover used in various figurative senses. Cp. *The Mad Lover*, i. 2. vol. vi. p. 137 :—

'*Calis.* Mark how he muses.
Lucip. H'as *a battalia now in's brains*; he *draws out.*'

The Nice Valour, v. 1. vol. x. p. 358 :—

'Away, receptacle
Of luxury and dishonour! most unfortunate
To make thyself but *lucky* to thy spoil,
After thy sex's manner.'

'Seward,' says Dyce, 'altered "lucky" to "*lackey*," explaining the line with that alteration to mean: "To make thyself a lackey, servant, or minister of thy own spoil"; and so the editors of 1778. Mason observes that the old text "may mean, You are most unfortunate in every attempt to redeem yourself, and lucky in more opportunities which conducted you to ruin." "Lackey" suggests to my mind no meaning whatsoever; and in the kind of explanation the editor gives it, he has entirely overlooked the word "*but*" before "*lucky*" which must be attended to.'

Mason's explanation is possibly the right one, and the oxymoron, 'unfortunate to make thyself lucky,' may be intentional; but I doubt the phrase 'to make thyself lucky,' and think we should read *lusty*, *i.e.* to deck yourself up for your own ruin. Compare *The Humorous Lieutenant*, ii. 2 :—

> 'And you shall see us all like sacrifices,
> In our best trim, fill up the mouth of ruin,'

a passage borrowed from *i. H. iv.* iv. 1. 113. The confusion of *st* and *ck* is not uncommon.

The Bloody Brother, iii. 1. vol. x. p. 413 :—

> 'Who knows not all things holy are prevented
> With ends of all impiety? all but
> Lust, gain, ambition.'

I think we should read,

> 'With ends of all impiety? *all* : but
> Lust, gain, ambition——'

all emphasising his statement, and the next sentence being broken off by Rollo's sudden entrance.

The Bloody Brother, iv. 1. vol. x. p. 431 :—

'Set not forth your leg
Of haste, nor put your face of business on ;
An honester affair than this I urge to,
You will not easily think on ; and 'twill be
Reward to entertain it. 'Tis your fortune
To have our master's ear above the rest
Of us that follow him ; *but that no one envies ;
For I have well consider'd truth* sometimes
May be conveyèd by the same conduits
That falsehood is.'

Heath (*MS. Notes*) explains, 'but that confidence no one envies you ; for I (and others too) have well considered, that truth,' etc., and Dyce approves the explanation. But we have nothing to indicate the insertion of 'and others too'; and even if we had authority for it, there seems to me no just sequence of ideas. I believe that the words ''Tis your fortune ... envies' are merely parenthethical, that an aposiopesis should be marked after 'entertain it,' and the sense be made to run on with the words 'For I,' etc.

The Night Walker, iii. 6. vol. xi. p. 175 :—

'*Ha legs!* what, does her speag hard urds to her, to make poor Guennith ridicles? was no mannerly sentilman to abuse her.'

Dyce notes, 'So the folio of 1679 (" Ha leggs "). The 4tos " Haleggs." See the conclusion of Maria's next speech.'

This reference is to me the strangest of explanations. Maria there says, 'Yet in her own countries was held a fine ense [wench], her can tell her, and honest ense too, marg you dat now : *her can keep her little legs close enough*, warrant her'; which is nothing more than a confirmation of her assertion that she was an 'honest (*i.e.* chaste) wench.' I take *Haleggs*, the reading of the quartos, to be Maria's Welsh for *Alack*, she pretending that Heartlove had spoken severely to her. All her *k*'s are, Welsh-like, *g*'s; and in every line she pluralises words, *e.g.* 'Londons,' 'seeze and butters,' 'ales and breds,' 'unders and mazements,' 'be her defences,' 'prain pans,' etc., etc.

Love's Pilgrimage, iii. 2. vol. xi. p. 277 :—

> 'But I shall find her out, with all her witchcrafts,
> Her paintings and her pouncings : for 'tis art,
> And only art preserves her, and mere spells
> That work upon his powers. Let her but show me
> A *ruin'd* cheek like mine, that holds his colour
> (And writes but sixteen years) in spite of sorrows,
> An unbath'd body, smiles that give but shadows,
> And wrinkle not the face!'

Surely *ruin'd* cannot be right here; a '*ruin'd* cheek' could not be said to 'hold his colour.' Leocadia, it is true, speaks of her sorrows as having somewhat marred her beauty :—

> 'No, sir, I hold my beauty
> (Wash but these sorrows from it) of a sparkle
> As right and rich as hers,'

but in the present speech she is emphasising the

freshness of her beauty in contrast with that of Theodosia. I believe we should read *rubi'd*, *i.e. rubied.*

The Two Noble Kinsmen, i. 4. vol. xi. p. 351 :—

> 'Since I have known fight's fury, friends' behests,
> Love's provocations, zeal in a mistress' task,
> Desire of liberty, a fever, madness,
> Hath set a mark which Nature could not reach to
> Without some imposition, sickness in will,
> Or wrestling strength in reason.'

Littledale explains 'which Nature . . . imposition' as meaning 'which could only be combated by practising some deception.' I cannot believe this to be the sense; but take it to be that 'fight's fury,' etc., have marked a man in a way that would have been impossible in the natural order of things unless there had been in his case some superinduced cause, such as weakness of will or severe mental struggle.

PEELE[1]

The Arraignment of Paris, i. 1. 84:—

> 'Her trailing tresses that hang flaring round,
> Of *July-flowers* so graffed in the ground.'

Bullen notes: 'Qy. carnations? Cf. Drayton's *Polyolbion*, song xv:—

> "The brave carnation then, of sweet and sovereign power
> (So of his colour called, although a *July-flower*)."'

I do not understand the query. *July-flower* is nothing more than another spelling of *gillofer*, our modern *gilly-flower* or carnation.

The Arraignment of Paris, iii. 1. 121:—

> 'His 'ticing curlèd hair, his front of ivory,
> Then had not I, poor I, bin unhappy.'

'Mr. P. A. Daniel,' says Bullen, 'suggests "poor I unhappy bin," which destroys the last vestige of rhyme.'

But neither Bullen nor Daniel seems to have noticed that the question is settled beyond dispute by ll. 73, 74, of *The Tale of Troy*:—

> 'His 'ticing curlèd hair, his front of ivory,
> The careless nymph had ne'er been so unhappy.'

---

[1] The references are to Bullen's edition, 2 vols., 1888.

Edward I. sc. iii. 39-41 :—

> 'Then, nobles, since you all agree in one,
> That for a crown so disagree in all,
> Since what I do shall rest irrevocable,
> *And lovely England, to thy lovely Queen,*
> *Lovely Queen Elinor, unto her turn thy eye,*
> *Whose honour cannot but love thee well;*
> Hold up your hands in sight, with general voice,
> That are content to stand to our award.'

That lines 39-41 are corrupt was seen by Dyce. Bullen further pointed out that they are misplaced. The scene in question is that in which, after his coronation, Edward gives his decision between the several competitors for the Scottish crown; and this speech is addressed to them upon Baliol's announcing their agreement to accept his award in the matter. Its drift is entirely arrested by the italicised lines, and the only question is to what place they should be transferred. Now, after Edward has made his award, Elinor, ll. 69-73, thus addresses Baliol :—

> 'Now, brave John Baliol, Lord of Galloway,
> And King of Scots, shine with thy golden head;
> Shake [thou] thy spears, in honour of his name,
> Under whose royalty thou wear'st the same.'

Immediately after these lines we have the stage direction, 'Queen Elinor's *Speech*,' a direction altogether unnecessary if that speech followed continuously upon the words just quoted, but necessary if, as I believe, Edward here reciprocates the compliment his Queen has paid him. Elinor calls upon Baliol to do honour to the name of Edward; Edward, in his turn, calls upon England to do honour to Elinor. I would, then, place ll. 39-41 here, emending them as follows :—

> 'And, *loyal* England, to thy lovely Queen,
> Lovely Queen Elinor, unto her turn thy eye,
> Whose honour cannot *choose* but *like* thee well,'

i.e. whom you cannot but be glad to honour. The insertion of *choose* is Dyce's suggestion. Before becoming aware of it I proposed *help* ; but *choose* is decidedly better as being more Elizabethan.

Edward I. sc. iii. 81 :—

> 'The welkin, spangled through with golden spots,
> Reflects no finer on a frosty night
> Than lovely Longshanks in his Elinor's eye :
> So, Ned, thy Nell in every part of thee,
> Thy person's guarded with a troop of Queens,
> And every Queen as brave as Elinor,
> Give glory to the glorious crystal quarries,
> Where every *robe* an object entertains
> Of rich device and princely majesty.'

This (as it stands) very obscure speech by Queen Elinor is addressed to Edward, clad in the suit of glass which she had provided for his coronation ceremony. The lines, 'So, Ned, ... Elinor,' apparently mean that she is reflected any number of times in the mirror of this suit of glass, and so he seems to be guarded by a troop of queens each as splendidly dressed as herself.

But for *robe* I believe we should read *orbe* (orb) = panel, *i.e.* these glorious crystal squares, every panel of which contains the image of her brave attire. As an archæological term *orb* is a blank window or panel; and the transposition of *robe* for *orbe* is made the more likely by the subject being one of dress.

Edward I. sc. iii. 93 :—

> 'On thee, sweet Ned, it shall become thy Nell
> Bounteous to be unto the beauteous :
> *O'er-pry the palms*, sweet fountains of my bliss,
> And I will stand on tiptoe for a kiss.'

The 'sweet fountains of' her 'bliss' are, no doubt, Edward's lips; a few lines above she says :—

> 'From forth whose coral lips I suck the sweet
> Wherewith are dainty Cupid's caudles made.'

But *O'er-pry the palms* is absolute nonsense. I would read, *O'er breathe your balm* : compare *Othello*, v. 2. 16 :—

> 'Ah, *balmy breath*, that dost almost persuade
> Justice to break her sword' :

and Greene, *Looking-Glass*, etc., p. 137/1, ed. Dyce :—

> 'Meanwhile my *balm* shall from thy *breath* arise.'

As *pry* would in Peele's day be written *prie*, the likeness of *breathe* to *prie the* would be considerable; and, the mistake once made, the omission of *your* would naturally follow.

Edward I. sc. iii. 95 :—

> 'He had no thought of any gentle heart
> That would not *seize* desire for such desart.'

For *seize* Dyce suggests *feel*, which does not seem to me at all in keeping with the context. The sense we require is this: He must be utterly wanting in all gentle thought who would not gratify desire for what is so well deserved, *i.e.* for the kiss Elinor had asked. I think we should read *ease*, as a verb. The words *seize* and *cease* are constantly written for each other in the old dramatists, and if *ease* had been mistaken for *cease*, that word might have then been altered to *seize*.

Edward I. sc. iii. 107-114 :—

> 'Brother of Scotland, you shall to your home,
> And live in honour there fair England's friend,—
> And thou, sweet Nell, Queen of King Edward's heart,
> *Shall now* come lesser at thy dainty love,
> *And* at coronation meet *thy* loving peers,
> When storms are past, and we have cool'd the rage
> Of these rebellious Welshmen, that contend
> 'Gainst England's majesty and Edward's crown.'

Surely there is considerable corruption here, though both Dyce and Bullen pass the lines by without comment. For what possible sense can there be in Edward's telling his Queen that she 'shall *now* come lesser at' her 'dainty love, when storms are past,' etc.? What sense in saying that she shall 'at coronation meet' her 'loving peers,' seeing that the coronation is over, and that she has no peers? To me it seems plain that l. 111, which as it stands is unmetrical, has been shuffled out of its place, and that there are at least four corruptions. I would read the passage thus:—

> 'Brother of Scotland, you shall to your home,
> At coronation meet *your* loving peers,
> And live in honour there fair England's friend.
> And thou, sweet Nell, Queen of King Edward's heart,
> *Shalt not* come lesser at thy dainty love
> When storms are past,' etc.

In scene ix. 1-3, Baliol's coronation is spoken of as having taken place, and he is there with his peers:—

> *Baliol.* Lords of Albania, and my peers in France,
> Since Baliol is invested in his rights,
> And wears the royal Scottish diadem,' etc.

The words 'come lesser,' l. 110, are perhaps suspicious, though capable of interpretation.

Edward I. sc. vii. 91, 92:—

> 'It is enough *Jove* change his glittering robes
> To see Mnemosyne and *the flies*.'

'The text,' says Bullen, 'is horribly corrupt. Mnemosyne was the mother of the Muses by Jupiter (see Apollodorus). Is it possible that Peele wrote—

> "To woo the mother of the Muses nine";

and that the word "Mnemosyne" is a marginal note imported into the text? A proper name may perhaps be concealed under "the flies." Mitford proposed :—

> "It is enough. Jove changes glittering robes
> And then he flies to see Mnemosyne."'

Neither of these conjectures seems to me to be at all in keeping with the context. For the last twenty lines or so Mortimer has been considering his chances of winning Elinor away from Lluellen, and in the latter ten of these twenty he comforts himself with the assurance that gold and eloquence and ease are temptations sufficient to purchase any woman's love, and to lure her from her lover if in desperate case, as Lluellen is. What has *Jove* to do in such a matter? That word and *Love* are frequently misprinted for each other, and I feel sure that this has happened here. I would therefore read :—

> 'It is enough *Love* change his glittering robes
> To *scare* Mnemosyne, and *then she* flies.'

i.e. the change from prosperity to adversity is enough in matters of love to scare away all memory of what has been, to blow to the winds all former vows of constancy: an expectation which earlier in the scene Elinor has falsified by declaring that no change of fortune shall ever induce her to forsake Lluellen.

Edward I. sc. x. 85-90 :—

' *Lancaster.* I had forgot to ask your majesty,
How do you with the *abbeys* here in Wales?
Longsh. As kings with rebels, Mun; our right prevails.
We have good Robin Hood and Little John,
The Friar and the *good* Maid Marian :
Why *our* Lluellen is a mighty man.'

The whole passage seems to me corrupt; though, except that Bullen questions *abbeys*, it is passed over by the editors. Robin Hood, Little John, Friar Tuck, and Maid Marian are the names assumed by Lluellen, Rice, Friar David, and Elinor, while wandering in the forest; *and as yet Edward has not been able to come upon them.* I would read :—

' *Lancaster.* I had forgot to ask your majesty
How do you with the *rabble* here in Wales?
Longsh. As kings with rebels, Mun·; our right prevails.
Why, *tho'* Luellen is a mighty man,
We'll have good Robin Hood and Little John,
The Friar, and the *fair* Maid Marian.'

Just below we have ' Robin's *rabble,*' and in sc. xii. 71, ' Robin and his *rabble.*'

Edward I. sc. xi. 1-8 :—

'*Enter* [Jack] *the* Novice *and his company to give the* Queen *music at her tent.*
Jack. Come, fellows, cast yourselves even round in a string—a ring I would say ; come, merrily on my word, for

the Queen is most liberal, and if you please her well, she will pay you royally; *so, lawful to brave well thy British lustily* to solace *our good Queen; God save her grace, and give our young prince a carpell in their kind!* Come on, come on, set your crowds, and beat your heads together, and behave you handsomely.

[*Here they sing and then exeunt.*

Of the words 'so, lawful . . . kind!' Dyce remarks, 'Of this I can make nothing satisfactory.' Bullen contents himself with suggesting *brawl* for *brave*.

I would read, '*Sòl, la, mi, fa! to't! raise* your British *voices* lustily to solace our good Queen, God save her grace, and give our young prince a *carol* in their kind!' In *solace* I take it there is a pun on *sol, la*; and my conjecture here receives support from a stage direction in *The Arraignment of Paris*, after l. 124 of Act v.: 'The music soundeth, and the Nymphs within sing or *solfa with voices and instruments* awhile,' the instruments here being their 'crowds,' *i.e.* fiddles. The word *well*, in l. 4, I believe, to have been caught from 'please her *well.*' As to *carpell*, though Murray, *English Dictionary*, gives *carpell*, s.v. *carpel, i.e.* 'one of the divisions or cells of the compounded pistil or fruit,' I feel convinced that the word is nothing more than a misprint of *carrell*, one of the many forms in the sixteenth century of the modern *carol*. For 'in their kind,' = as befits such personages, cf. sc. i. 173 : 'There, my lord; neither one, two, nor three, but a poor cipher in agrum to enrich good fellows, and compound their figure *in their kind.*'

Edward I. sc. xii. 155 :—

' I must lop his longshanks, 'fore I'll *ear* to a pair of longshanks.'

The words are spoken by Lluellen before engaging in combat with Edward (Longshanks); and *ear* is evidently corrupt. Brinsley Nicholson proposes *lower.* I would read *carve,* in the sense of do homage to, show deference to. For the word in this sense, cp. Beaumont's *Remedy of Love,* Beaumont and Fletcher's works, ed. Dyce, vol. xi. p. 483 :—

' Salute him friendly, give him gentle words,
  Return all courtesies that he affords;
  Drink to him, *carve* him, give him compliment ' :

and see Dyce, *Glossary to Shakespeare,* s.v. Here I believe Lluellen is playing upon the words *lop* and *carve.*

Edward I. sc. xviii. 8 :—

'And now since, like one of Mars his *frozen* knights, I must hang up my weapon upon this tree,' etc.'

'"Qy. *chosen,*" says the editor of Dodsley's O. P.? But perhaps Peele alludes to some incident in some romance."—Dyce. There may be an allusion to the gladiators' custom of hanging up their weapons, when they retired from their profession, as a votive offering to the patron deity. "Frozen"=numbed with age' (Bullen).

There is no doubt an allusion to the hanging up of arms in this way; but the custom was not peculiar to gladiators. Knights in the Middle Ages frequently hung up their arms in churches, cathedrals, etc., when their career was run (cf. *e.g.* Archas, in *The Loyal Subject*, and the conspirators in *The White Devil*, who pretend to do so); and here I would read *proven* for *frozen*, a term frequently applied to knights of established reputation.

Edward I. sc. xxv. 9 :—

'*Queen Elinor.* Ah, Joan, I perish through a double war.
First in this painful prison of my soul,
A world of dreadful *sins holp thee* to fight,
And nature having lost her working power,
Yields up her earthly fortunes unto death.
Next of a war my soul is over-preased,
In that my conscience loaded with mis deeds,
Sits seeing my confusion to ensue,
Without especial favour from above.'

For *holp thee* Collier gives *holp here*; Dyce, *holp there*; while Bullen suggests *hale me*: none of them, in my opinion, satisfactory emendations. Moreover, none of the commentators notices *sins*, which I feel sure is corrupt. Elinor is speaking of a double warfare, that going on in her body, 'this painful prison of my soul' (as Bullen notices, and for which we may compare *King John*, iii. 4,

17-19), and that going on in her soul. What then, in the former of these conflicts can *sins* have to do? I would read :—

'A world of dreadful *foes bold them* to fight.'

'Nature,' as she goes on to say, 'having lost her working power,' can no longer struggle against these foes, but gives up the fight and dies. For the verb *bold*, here used reflexively, compare *Lear*, v. 1. 27, 'It toucheth us, as France invades our land, Not *bolds* the King.' In *All's Well*, iii. 2. 93, we have,

'This fellow has a deal of that too much
Which *holds* him much to have,'

and there Addis and Jervis both conjecture *bolds*, —a conjecture I myself had made many years before it appeared in *The Cambridge Shakespeare*. For a struggle similar to that of Elinor, compare *Julius Cæsar*, ii. 1. 67-69, though there the struggle is of the powers of the soul.

Edward I. sc. xxv. 18 :—

'Subdue your fever by *precious* art,
And help you still through hope of heavenly aid.'

For *precious*, Bullen queries *religious* or *religion's*. But Joan is referring to the two different kinds of suffering of which Elinor has just complained, her physical and her moral malady. I would therefore read '*physician's* art.' In the *Merry Wives of Windsor*, ii. 1. 5, all the old editions have *precisians* where *physicians* is now generally read.

Edward I. sc. xxv. 29 :—

> 'So thou, poor soul, may tell a *servile* tale,
> May counsel me; but I that prove the pain
> May hear thee talk but not redress my harm.'

For *servile*, Bullen proposes *suasive* or *soothing*. I would read *civil*, *i.e.* decorously comforting, platitudinous.

Edward I. sc. xxv. 70 :—

> 'Whose love comparèd with my loose delights,
> With many sorrows *that* my soul affrights.'

As Dyce says, 'the couplet, as it now stands, is nonsense.' Qy. 'with many sorrows *black*,' etc.?

Edward I. sc. xxv. 113 :—

> 'Pyropus' harden'd *flames* did ne'er reflect
> More hideous flames than from my breast arise.'

Here 'hardened flames' *may* mean substance looking like concreted flames. The pyrope was both a precious stone (a kind of garnet), and also a metallic composition, gold-bronze, made by adding six scruples of gold, or one quarter, to the ounce of copper (see Munro on Lucretius, ii. 803); and here as the passage is clearly an allusion to Ovid, *Met.* ii. 2, Clara micante auro, flammasque imitante pyropo, the metallic composition seems to be intended. But I am inclined to read 'harden'd *veins*,' 'flames' being caught from the line below.

Edward I. sc. xxv. 118, 120:—

'O, that those eyes that lighten'd *Cæsar's brain*,
O, that those looks that master'd Phœbus brand,
Or else those *looks* that stain Medusa's far,
Should shrine deceit, desire, and lawless lust.'

Medusa's is Collier's certain correction of *Melisaes*, but *looks* should undoubtedly be changed to *locks*, for it was by her golden hair that Medusa captivated Neptune; and the mistake here is due to *looks* in the previous line. Dyce queries this, and quotes from *The Arraignment of Paris*, i. 2. 24:—

'How Phorcys wife, that was so trick and fair,
That tangled Neptune in her golden hair':

a passage that escaped me when these conjectural readings were first published. For *Cæsar's brain* I should like to read *Ceres' brow*, supposing *brain* to be caught from *brand* in the next line. The three similes will then be all taken from mythology. A friend suggests that Peele was thinking of the *vegeti oculi* ascribed to Cæsar by Suetonius: but would the poet liken Elinor's eyes to those of a man, however lively they might be?

Edward I. sc. xxv. 182:—

'Ay, but when ladies list to run astray,
The poor supposèd father wears the horn,
And *pleating* leave their *liege* in princes' laps.'

'Mitford,' says Bullen, ' proposed :—

> "Ay, but when ladies list to run astray,
> And leave their plighted liege in princes' laps,
> The poor supposèd father wears the horn."

But the text would still be wretchedly unintelligible. The transposition of lines 181-2 is, I think, right. For "pleating" I would read "fleeting"; but the rest of the verse is unmanageable. Qy. "and fleeting leave their liege lord's princely bed?" (Very unsatisfactory).'

Accepting Mitford's transposition and Bullen's conjecture *fleeting*, I would read :—

> 'And *fleeting* leave their *siege* in princes' laps,'

the word *siege* being used, as it frequently is, for *seat, place, position*; with perhaps an allusion to the term as technically applied to a heron who, when disturbed while watching for her prey, is said to be put from her *siege*.

Edward I. sc. xxv. 269 :—

> 'Pale death, alas, hath banished all thy pride,
> *Thy* wedlock-vows.'

Qy. 'all thy pride *Of* wedlock-vows,' *Thy* being caught from the next line, 'Thy eyes, thy looks, thy lips,' etc.?

The Battle of Alcazar, i. (The Presenter's Address), 21 :—

> '*Like* those that *were* by kind of murder *mumd*,
> Sit down and see what heinous stratagems

> These damnèd wits contrive ; and lo, alas,
> How like poor lambs prepared for sacrifice,
> This traitor-king hales to their longest home
> These tender lords, his younger brethren both.'

For *mumd* Daniel conjectures *numb'd*, and, influenced, I suppose, by this suggestion, Bullen for *down* in the next line queries *dumb*; while, rightly feeling the awkwardness of *kind* in such a context, he queries *sight* for that word.

But, with all these alterations, I fail to find any sense in the passage ; nor do I see why the Presenter should prescribe to the audience how they were to sit. On the other hand, I do understand why, when the murder of the boys is to be performed on the stage, the Presenter should apologise for such violation of the Horatian precept ; and I would read,

> '*Let* those that *are* by kind of murder *fond*,
> Sit down,' etc. :

i.e. let those who are by nature fond of witnessing murderous spectacles, sit, etc.

The Battle of Alcazar, i. 2. 38, 39 :—

> ' *The Bassa grossly flatter'd to his face,*
> *And Amurath's praise advanced above the clouds ;*
> Upon the plains the soldiers being spread,
> And that great guard of sturdy janizaries
> That Amurath to Abdelmelec gave,
> And bade him boldly be with them as safe
> As if he slept within a wallèd town ;
> Who take them to their weapons, threatening revenge
> Bloody revenge, bloody revengeful war.'

Conjectural Readings

The two first lines should come at the end of the speech, with a comma only after *war*. Without this transposition the passage has neither sense nor grammatical construction; and the Moor's answer plainly shows the necessity.

The Battle of Alcazar, i. 2. 54:—

'Sith they begin to bathe [their swords] in blood,
Blood be the theme whereon our time shall *tread*.'

'This line,' says Bullen, 'is very corrupt.' Qy. " Blood be the theme *whereof our stile shall treat*."? The emendation would give a grimly jocular turn to the line. The "stile" (Lat. stilus) would be cold steel.'

A much simpler alteration would be *read* for *tread*, a word which may have been due to the *-on* in *whereon*.

The Battle of Alcazar, ii. 4. 19:—

'These lines, my lord, writ in extremity,
Contain therefore but during fortune's date.'

'There must,' says Bullen, 'be some corruption here. Qy. "Contain *their force* but," etc.' I see no need of emendation, for *contain* was of old sometimes used for *continue, endure*.

The Battle of Alcazar, ii. 4. 120, 121:—

'Both nature, time, and fortune all agree
To bless and serve her royal majesty.
The wallowing ocean hems her round about;
Whose raging floods do swallow up her foes

> And on the rocks their ships in pieces split,
> And even in Spain, *where* all the *traitors* dance
> And *play* themselves upon a sunny day,
> Securely guard the west part of her isle.'

The passage is part of a long panegyric of Elizabeth and England spoken by King Sebastian of Portugal. Bullen thus annotates: 'Dyce makes no comment here; but it is plain that this line and the next are hideously corrupt. We should put a full stop after "split" (l. 119); and some reckless emendator might then propose:—

> "Th' Atlantic main, where gayly dolphins dance
> And 'joy themselves upon the sunny wave,
> Securely guards," etc.

Very far from the original; but the original is nonsense.'

Reckless indeed! I think in the first place that there is a clear allusion to the defeat of the Spanish Armada, 1588, an allusion that would be apt enough in a play published in 1594, and probably, according to Dyce, in existence as early as February 1591-2. There is, I believe, the same allusion in *Cymbeline*, iii. i. 26-29, though the Queen is there speaking of Cæsar's invasion:—

> '... his shipping—
> Poor ignorant baubles!—on our terrible seas,
> Like egg-shells moved upon their surges, crack'd
> As easily 'gainst our rocks.'

In the second place, I believe that the corruption

is not so much in the words of ll. 120, 121, as in the omission of a line after *split*, and of another, such as I have suggested in order to show the construction, after l. 121. I propose to substitute *there* for *where*, *tritons* for *traitors*, and *splay* for *play* : the lines would then run :—

> 'Whose raging floods do swallow up her foes,
> And on the rocks their ships in pieces split,
>
> .   .   .   .   .
>
> And even in Spain : *there* all the *tritons* dance
> And *splay* themselves upon a sunny day,
> [The tutelary deities that from harm]
> Securely guard the west part of her isle.'

With the words 'there all . . . day' we may compare *Antony and Cleopatra*, v. 8. 88-90 :—

> '. . . his delights
> Were dolphin-like ; they show'd his back above
> The element they lived in' :

and *Friar Bacon and Friar Bungay*, sc. viii. 57-59 :—

> 'Like Thetis shalt thou wanton on the waves,
> And draw the dolphins to thy lovely eyes,
> To dance lavoltas in the purple streams':

and, as in the following lines of the passage, Neptune and Venus are spoken of as frequenting, and throwing their protection over, the seas to the south and east of England, we need some deities like the tritons to do the same office for the west. For *splay*=display, compare Gascoigne's Works (quoted by Nares), 'Let bring his banners *splaide*,' and again, ' Our ensigns *splayde*.' So, too, *Hickscorner*, l. 19, '*Splayed* on a crow.' Possibly the mention of the tritons and Neptune is a reminiscence of Vergil *Æn*. v. 817, etc.; Venus of course being given her part as having risen from the sea.

The Battle of Alcazar, v. i. 9-11 :—

> ' My lord, when *with our ordnance fierce we sent*
> Our Moors with smaller shot, as thick as hail
> Follows apace, to charge the Portugal ;
> The valiant Duke, the devil of Avero, . . .
> Breaks through the ranks, and,' etc.

' The text,' says Bullen, ' is corrupt. I suggest the following emendation :—

> " My lord, when *we our ordnance force had spent*,
> Our Moors with smaller shot, as thick as hail,
> Follows [*i.e.* follow] apace." '

The emendation is a taking one; but there is this objection to it, that we lose the connection with the lines immediately following. Possibly with a comma only after ' Portugal,' the sense may be, ' When together with our heavy artillery, with which we plied them, we sent our Moors with shot, poured forth with the rapidity of hail, to charge,' etc. The word ' charge ' is not necessarily used here in the commoner sense of rushing upon the enemy with sword, bayonet, etc., but may mean merely to attack, assail.

The Battle of Alcazar, v. 1. 37 :—

> 'His honours and his *types* he hath resign'd.'

Here and in l. 211,

> 'With all allegiance and with honour's *types*,'

I am inclined to read *styles*: in both cases, it may be noticed, the word follows one ending in *s*.

The Battle of Alcazar, v. 1. 252 :—

> 'His skin we will be parted from his flesh,
> And being stiffenèd *and* stuff'd with straw,
> So to deter and fear the lookers-on
> From any such foul fact or bad attempt.'

'After these words [*i.e.* "stuff'd with straw"], a line,' says Dyce (about the stuffed skin being set up in some conspicuous place) is certainly wanting.'

I rather doubt this, and think that if we substitute *be* for *and*, in l. 252, we shall get the idea of the scarecrow being set up.

David and Bethsabe, sc. i. 67 :—

> 'Bright Bethsabe gives *earth* to my desires,
> Verdure to earth, and to that verdure flowers.'

'This word,' says Bullen, 'is suspicious; but Collier's correction "birth" is not happy.' The word is not merely 'suspicious,' but manifestly corrupt. I would read *warmth*.

David and Bethsabe, sc. 1. 85 :—

> 'My lord the king, elect to God's own heart
> Should not His gracious jealousy incense
> Whose thoughts are chaste : *I* hate incontinence.'

'Daniel,' says Bullen, 'suggests *and* for *I*': rather, I think, *ay*, which was of old so often written *I*; with a comma only after 'chaste.'

David and Bethsabe, sc. i. 106, 115 :—

'*David.* Welcome, fair Bethsabe, King David's darling.
Thy *bones' fair covering*, erst discovered *fair*,
And all mine eyes with all thy beauties pierced.
As heaven's bright eye burns most when most he climbs
The crooked zodiac with his fiery sphere,
And shineth furthest from his earthly globe ;
So since thy beauty scorch'd my conquered soul,
I called thee nearer for my nearer cure.
Beth. Too near, my lord, was your unarmed heart
When furthest off my hapless beauty pierced ;
And would this *dreary* day had turned to night,
Or that some pitchy cloud had cloaked the sun,
Before their lights had caused my lord to see
His name disparaged and my chastity.'

On l. 107 Bullen remarks, ' By reading " Enthrall'd mine eyes," we could make some sense of this corrupt passage.'

I believe the corruption is not here, but in the previous line. David's simile is in effect this : ' As the sun's rays scorch most fiercely when he is furthest from the earth, so, when formerly you were far from me, the beams of your beauty most scorched my heart ; and therefore I summoned you to me in the hope that, when near me, your beauty would less inflame me.' To this simile I see no pertinence in the words 'Thy bones' fair covering, erst discovered fair'; nor can I believe that Peele, even in his most turgid mood, would speak of her 'bones' fair covering' as 'piercing' the eye. I would read,

'Thy *beams far hovering* erst discovered *fire*';

putting a comma only after 'pierced': *fair*, I imagine, was caught from the line above, and the copyist ingeniously found a play of words in 'covering' and 'discovered.' For *dreary*, l. 115, Bullen suggests *garish*; I should prefer *fiery*, a reference to David's words. Compare also, for the whole passage, Bethsabe's words, ll. 7-10:—

'Let not my *beauty's fire*
Inflame unstaid desire,
Nor *pierce* any bright eye,
That wandereth lightly:'

and those of David ll. 26-27:—

'What tunes, what words, what looks, what wonders *pierce*
My soul incensed with a sudden *fire*.'

David and Bethsabe, sc. iii. 95:—

'To figure Amnon's *resting* cruelty,
And tragic spoil of Tamar's chastity.'

Bullen notes, 'There seems to be some corruption here; but "resting" may be used in the sense of lasting. (Qy. "wresting"?).'

I would read *resty*, *i.e.* rank. Cotgrave gives

'*Ranci*: Musty, fusty, reasie, *resty*, tainted, . . . putrified . . . stinking, unsavoury, ill-smelling': '*Relant*: Musty, fusty, *resty*, reasie, dankish, unsavoury': and Minsheu: '*Resty*, rank.'

David and Bethsabe, sc. iii. 137:—

> 'Smite, David, deadlier than the voice of heaven,
> And let hate's fire *be kindled* in thy heart:
> *Frame* in the arches of thy angry brows,
> Making thy forehead, like a comet, shine,
> To force false Amnon tremble at thy looks.'

Read, without doubt :—

> 'And let hate's fire, *be-kindled* in thy heart,
> *Flame* in the arches of thy angry brows,' etc.

What sense the editors may have found in framing in the sockets of the eyes, I am quite unable to guess.

David and Bethsabe, sc. v. 26:—

> 'There came a stranger to this wealthy man;
> And he refused and spared to take his own;
> Or of his store to dress and make him meat,
> But took the poor man's sheep, *partly*, poor man's store,
> And dressed it for this stranger in his house.'

Bullen remarks 'The text is hopelessly corrupt.' Not 'hopelessly,' I think. I would read :—

> 'But took the poor man's sheep, *pardy, the* poor man's store':

i.e. the poor man's sheep, or, by God, I might

say the poor man's whole store, for this ewe lamb was all he had. Peele is fond of this oath, 'pardy' or 'perdy.'

David and Bethsabe, sc. viii. 106 :—

> 'O thou, that hold'st his raging *bloody bound*
> Within the circle of the silver moon,
> That girds earth's centre with his watery scarf,
> Limit the counsel of Achitophel.'

Bullen remarks, 'Very corrupt. Qy. "sea's ranging body bound"? That *raging* is a misprint for *ranging* I am convinced; but the rest is dark.' Read:—

> 'O thou, that hold'st his raging *flood y-bound*':

with the sense, 'O thou, that holdest bound within the circle of the silver moon the raging flood of him that girds,' etc., or, in plain prose, 'O thou, that by the moon's influence controllest the tides,' etc. Compare *The Battle of Alcazar*, iii. 4. 118 :—

> 'Whose *raging floods* do swallow up her foes.'

As *y-bound* here, so in *The Tale of Troy* Peele writes *y-clypped, y-blinded*; in *An Eclogue Gratulatory, y-born, y-comen*; in *Polyhymnia, y-clad*.

David and Bethsabe, sc. xi. 13 :—

> 'Making huge floods upon the land I leave
> To ravish *them* and all their fairest fruits.'

Bullen says that by *them* are to be understood

Achitophel's countrymen. Surely not; the word refers to *land*, which it is hardly necessary to pluralise. So, in the next couplet, he prays that his sighs may hang upon 'his hedges like eternal mists.'

Sir Clyomon and Sir Clamydes, sc. xi. 96 :—

'If your grace, O noble dame, will so accept of me.'

Qy. 'If *that* your grace,' etc., or is *your* a dissyllable?

The Praise of Chastity, 43 :—

'Believe me, to contend 'gainst armies royal,
  To tame wild panthers but by strength of hand,
To praise *the* triumph, not so special,
  As 'ticing pleasure's charms for to withstand.'

'Unintelligible,' says Bullen. 'Qy. "raise"?'
This hardly mends matters, I think. The whole poem is on the *praise* due to chastity, and the essence of a real triumph. I would read :—

'To praise *of* triumph*'s* not so special :'

i.e. has no such special claim to the praise of having triumphed. Compare the immediately following stanzas :—

'And, for me list compare with men of war,
  For honour of the field, I dare maintain,
This victory exceedeth that as far
  As Phœbus' chariot Vulcan's forge doth stain.

Both noble, and *triumphant* in their kinds,
    And matter worthy Queen Remembrance' pen ;
But that that tangles both our thoughts and minds,
    To master that, is more than over men
To make thy triumph.'

Also the opening stanzas of the poem.

MARLOWE[1]

1. *Tamburlaine*, v. 1. 117 :—

'Techelles, straight go charge a few of them
  To *charge* these dames, and show my servant, death.'

I would read *take* : *charge* being caught from the previous line. Immediately afterwards Tamburlaine says :—

'Away with them, I say, and show them death,'

and the stage direction to the line is *The Virgins are taken out.*

1. *Tamburlaine*, v. 1. 183-187 :—

'I thus conceiving and subduing both
  That which hath stoopt the *chiefest* of the gods
  Even from the fiery-spangled veil of Heaven,
  To feel the lowly warmth of shepherd's flames,
  And mask in cottages of *strowèd reeds.*'

'The 8vo,' says Bullen, 'reads :—

"That which hath *stopt* the *tempest* of the gods . . .
. . . . . .
And *martch* in cottages of strowed *weeds.*"

'The quarto makes matters worse by reading *march* in *coatches*. Broughton suggested *stoopt* for

[1] The references are to Bullen's edition, 3 vols. 1885.

stopt and *mask* for *martch*, but left *tempest*....'
The other alterations are Dyce's.

I would read :—

'That which hath stoopt the *topmost* of the gods ...

. . . . . .

And mask in cottages of *strawèd weeds*.'

It seems to me impossible that *chiefest* could ever have been corrupted into *tempest*; whereas if in *topmost* the *p* and *m* were transposed, we should at once have *tempest*, *e* and *o* being so constantly confused. It is true that *topmost* as applied to Jove would be a rather unusual epithet; but, the metaphor being taken from hawking, that epithet would not be inappropriate to the quarry that was soaring highest in the air. To *strawèd weeds* = *thatch*, I can see no objection; compare *As You Like It*, iii. 3. 11, 'worse than Jove in a thatch'd house'; and Marlowe's translation of Ovid's *Elegies*, ii. 9. 18 :—

'With *strawy* cabins now her court should build.'

In l. 183 I am inclined to suspect *both*, for it can there only mean 'moreover,' and in such a sense the position of the word is very strange.

1. *Tamburlaine*, v. 1. 236 :—

'And then shall we in this detested guise,
  With shame, with hunger, and with horror *stay*,
  Griping our bowels with retorquèd thoughts
  And have no hope to end our ecstasies.'

For *stay* the 8vo gives *aie*; the 4to *aye*. I think we should read *vie*, *i.e.* contend against. See note on *The Wild-Goose Chase*, i. 1., p. 72 above.

II. *Tamburlaine*, i. 3. 147 :—

'. . . as if infernal Jove

. . . . . .

Should pierce the black circumference of hell
With ugly Furies bearing fiery flags,
And millions of his strong tormenting spirits.
From *strong* Tesella unto Biledull
All Barbary is unpeopled for my sake.'

Dyce suspects *strong* in 'strong tormenting' (which, by the way, I would write 'strong-tormenting'). Rather, I think, the latter *strong* has been caught from the former, and I would read 'From *far* Tesella.'

II. *Tamburlaine*, iii. 2. 99 :—

'Hast thou beheld a peal of ordnance strike
A ring of pikes, mingled with *shot* and horse.'

Dyce conjectured *foot* for *shot*, though admitting that 'a ring of pikes' is the same as 'foot.' Mitford would read :—

'A ring of pikes and horse, *mangled* with shot.'

But *mangled* is discredited by the very next words, 'whose *shatter'd* limbs,' etc. I believe that *shot* is sound. The word was of old used for soldiers armed with guns, as contrasted with pikemen, and also for horse-soldiers, as in Peele's *Battle of Alcazar*, iv. 1. 57 :—

> 'Hamet, my brother, with a thousand *shot*
> On horseback.'

So, in *i. H. vi.* i. 4. 53, 'a guard of chosen *shot.*'

II. *Tamburlaine*, v. 3. 188 :—

> ' If not resolved into *resolved* pains.'

The latter *resolved* cannot, I think, be right, but must have been caught from the former. Amyras shortly afterwards prays heaven to send his soul the 'burning agony' from which his father is suffering, and some such word as 'burning' or 'torturing' is wanted here, the final syllable of *resolved* being accented.

II. *Tamburlaine*, v. 3. 199 :—

> 'Leading a life that only strives to die,
> And *plead* in vain unpleasing sovereignty.'

The word *plead* makes no sense. Bullen suspects that the true reading is *pleased.* But this gives no construction to the words 'unpleasing sovereignty.' I would read *wield*, supposing *plead* to be due to *leading* in the line above.

Faustus, Chorus, l. 2 :—

> 'Where Mars did *mate* the Carthaginians.'

For *mate* = associate with, compare *The Winter's Tale*, i. 2. 142 :—

> 'With what's unreal thou coactive art,
> And *fellow'st* nothing.'

It seems to me rather a gratuitous assumption to suppose with Ward and Bullen that Marlowe had forgotten that the Carthaginians were victorious; though of course *mate* in the sense of 'defeat,' 'confound,' is common enough.

The Jew of Malta, i. 1. 4 :—

'As for those *Samintes*, and the men of Uz,
  That bought my Spanish oils and wines of Greece,
  Here have I purst their paltry silverlings.'

For *Samintes* modern editors read *Samnites*. Bullen gives *Sabans*, and remarks: 'Between "Samnites" and the "men of Uz" there can be no possible connection. My emendation suits the context. We have Saba for Sabæa in *Faustus*, xii. 25, etc.' But surely *Sabans* is a very violent change, and there seems no other justification for it than the fact that the Sabæans are mentioned, *Job*, i. 15, as falling upon Job's herds. I would read *Samarites*. The enmity between the Jews and Samaritans would account for the scornful tone of Barabas's words; and as Uz, so far as its position has been ascertained, lay either east or south-east of Palestine, there would be nothing strange in its being associated by Marlowe with Samaria.

The Jew of Malta, i. 2. 383 :—

'Though *countermined* with walls of brass.'

Both here and in v. 3. 3, 'Strong-*countermined*

with other petty isles,' I would read 'counter-*mured*.' Murray, *English Dictionary*, quotes another instance of the misuse of 'counter*mine*' from R. Johnson's *Kingdom and Commonwealth*, 1630, but the misprint is so easy that I feel sure it has occurred in each case. Marlowe was not likely to make a blunder of this kind.

The Jew of Malta, ii. 1. 44 :—

'*Abig.* Then, father, here receive thy happiness.
                          [*Throws down bags.*
Bar. Hast thou't?
Abig. Here [*Throws down the bags*], hast thou't?
There's more, and more, and more.'

The words *Hast thou't?* in the mouth of Barabas seem to me quite out of place. I believe they belong to Abigail only, and are said by her in inquiry whether Barabas has caught the bags which in the dim light of the coming dawn she has thrown down. I would read :—

'Then, father, here receive thy happiness [*Throws down bags*] : hast thou't?
There's more, and more, and more.
                    [*Throws down* MORE *bags.*'

The second stage direction seems to me to require the insertion of the word *more.*

The Jew of Malta, iv. 1. 124 :—

'Therefore 'tis not requisite he should live.

Though such inversions are common enough

the rhythm of the line would be improved by reading :—

> 'Therefore *'tis requisite* he should *not* live.'

The Jew of Malta, iv. 4. 74 :—

> 'Go to, no more. I'll make him send me half he has, and
> Glad he scapes so. [*Pen and ink.*
> I'll write unto him ; we'll have money straight.'

The words *pen and ink*, which Dyce and Bullen print as a stage direction, stand in the original edition as part of the text ; and, I think, rightly so, they being Ithamore's call for writing materials. Compare Heywood, *If you know not me*, etc., vol. i. p. 314, Pearson's reprint :—

> '*Pen and ink!* I'll set it down in black and white.'

Dido, iii. 2. 3 :—

> 'Here lies my hate, Æneas cursed brat,
> The boy wherein false Destiny delights,
> *The heir of Fury*, the favourite of the Fates.'

'Heir of Fury,' says Bullen, 'is certainly a strange expression, but I dare not adopt Cunningham's emendation "heir of Troy."' *Troy* seems to me very tempting, but perhaps we should read :—

> '*Heir of the Furies*, favourite of the Fates.'

Dido, iv. 1. 4 :—

> '*Ach.* Did ever men see such a sudden storm
> Or day so clear so suddenly o'ercast ?
> *Jar.* I think some fell enchantress dwelleth here,
> That can call them forth whenas she please.'

Bullen suggests, 'That can *call forth the winds,*' etc. A lesser change would be '*One* that can call them,' etc., *them* referring to 'storms' implied in *storm*, l. 1.

Dido, iv. 5. 28 :—

'Especially in women of *your* years.'

Qy. *our?* She is not here apostrophising herself, and when she does, she uses *thou* and *thy*.

Dido, v. 1. 110 :—

'Then let me go, and never say farewell :
Let me go; farewell: I must from hence.'

'A word,' says Bullen, 'which it is not easy to supply has been omitted. Dyce's "farewell [none]," and Cunningham's "let me go *is* farewell," are equally unsatisfactory.'

I would read, 'Let me *forgo* farewell.' The copyist finding 'Let me go' in l. 109, carelessly repeated the words without reference to the sense and, as *forgo* would be written '*fore*go,' his blunder may have been helped by the first syllable of '*fare*well.'

Dido, v. 1. 221 :—

'Traitress too *keend* and cursèd sorceress.'

So the old editions. Dyce takes *keend* as ='kenned,' *i.e.* known, manifest. Qy. 'Traitress to *kind?*' *i.e.* to those of your own household.

Dido, v. 1. 276 :—

> 'Not far from hence
> There is a woman famousèd for arts,
> *Daughter* unto the nymphs Hesperides.'

Bullen notes, '*Daughter* is nonsense. Should we read "Guardian to" (or "unto")? Cf. Verg. *Æn.* iv. 484: "Hesperidum templi custos."' But, to say nothing of the violence of the alteration, surely there is a vast difference between 'guardian to the nymphs Hesperides' and 'guardian of the temple of the Hesperides.' Vergil's lines are :—

> 'Hinc mihi Massylae gentis monstrata sacerdos,
> Hesperidum templi custos, epulasque draconi
> Quae dabat, et sacros seruabat in arbore ramos,
> Spargens humida mella, soporiferumque papauer.'

There is no doubt a difficulty as to the last of these lines if applied to the care of the dragon by the priestess, an application which, however, does not seem to me a necessary one; but, whatever the exact sense here, that functionary dealt in drugs as well as charms; and when the funeral pile is erected, it is by her that

> 'Falcibus et messae ad Lunam quaeruntur aenis
> Pubentes herbae, nigri cum lacte ueneni ;
> Quaeritur et nascentis equi de fronte reuolsus
> Et matri praeraptus amor.'

I would therefore propose *drugster* for *daughter* ; the termination *-ster* being of old a feminine one.

Hero and Leander, First Sestiad, l. 477 :—

'And fruitful wits that *inaspiring* are.'

Bullen suggests '*high*-aspiring.' Perhaps we might read :—

'And wits that fruitful *in aspiring* are.'

Ovid's Elegies, iii. 7. 29 :—

'With virgin wax hath some *imbast* my joints?'

Dyce queries, 'Is this to be understood as *embasted* or as *embased*, impaired, relaxed?' Bullen takes the word in the latter sense.

Qy. *impaste. i.e.* impasted? Compare *Hamlet*, ii. 4. 281 :—

'   .   .   .   horridly trick'd,
With blood of fathers, mothers, daughters, sons,
Baked and *impasted* with the parching streets.   .

The Latin has, Sagave poenicea *defixit* nomina cera?

I may perhaps mention that in two conjectures I find myself anticipated, in one by Dyce, in the other by Steevens. On i. *Tamburlaine*, iii. 3. 158 :—

'And make your strokes to wound the senseless *light*,'

I had written, 'The old copies give *lure*. Surely we should read *air* : if the loop of the *a* in *aire* were open, the word would look very like *lure*. The idea is more poetically expressed in *Hamlet*, iv. 1. 44, "hit the woundless air."' On *The Jew of Malta*, iv. 6. 22, 'Snickle hand *too fast*,' my note was, 'I would read "Snickle hand *to fist*," *i.e.* each pulling hard at the end of the noose.' Heywood, I now find, uses the phrase in *The Witches of Lancashire*, v. 1. 6: 'Zooks, did I ever think that a godson of mine should have fought *hand to fist* with the devil!' The fact that these conjectures were made independently adds to the likelihood of their being sound.

CHAPMAN[1]

The Blind Beggar of Alexandria, vol. i. p. 5 :—

> 'To him that *succours* him, Ile threaten death,
> But he that doth not *threaten* him shall die,
> For who is worthy, life shall see him want.'

Read,

> 'To him that *threatens* him, I'll threaten death,
> But he that doth not *succour* him, shall die;
> For who is worthy life will see him want?'

The Blind Beggar of Alexandria, vol. i. p. 24 :—

> 'If I would let him have his statutes in,
> And take *other* assurance for another thousand.'

Omit *other*, comparing p. 27, 'and take assurance for another thousand.'

The Blind Beggar of Alexandria, vol. i. p. 29 :—

> 'Bright Nimph, I come in name of all the worlde,
> That now sustains dead winter in the spring,
> To have *a graces from thy summer* darted.'

Read,

> 'To have *a summer from thy graces* darted.'

---

[1] The references are to Pearson's Reprint, 3 vols., 1873.

An Humerous Dayes Mirth, vol. i. p. 54 :—

'Colenet you know no man better, that you are mightily in love with *love by* Martia daughter to old Foyes.'

Read,

'Colenet, you know, no man better, that you are mightily in love with *lovely* Martia, daughter, etc.'

An Humerous Dayes Mirth, vol. i. p. 58 :—

'Sure, my lord, if I thought I shold be rid of this same *banishment* of barrenes,' etc.

Read, *punishment;* and compare *The Malcontent*, iv. 2. 112, where *banishing* is misprinted for *publishing*.

All Fooles, vol. i. p. 143 :—

'*Val.* Toyes, toyes, a pox; and yet they be such toyes
As every gentleman would not be without.
Cor. Vayne glory makes yee judge *on tyte yfaith*.'

Read, *'em light, ifaith*.

All Fooles, vol. i. p. 150 :—

'And take um from their close deere holes, as *fat*
As a Phisician.'

Read, *pat*.

All Fooles, vol. i. p. 168 :—

'Their winckes, their beckes, *due gard*.'

Read, *dieu garde!*

Monsieur D'Olive, vol. i. p. 211 :—

'Your Grace, *tere his* time.'

Read, *ere this*; a correction which I give in order to remark that I shall not notice in their places such obvious misprints as *court* for *count*, *toples* for *topless*, *sonne* for *sun*, *saite* for *say it*, *fivers* for *fibres desolate* for *dissolute*, *yee* for *ice*, *curning* for *burning*, *rubers* for *rulers*, *must* for *most*, *iyrck* for *yerk*, *ter* for *after*, *haud* for *hand*, *start* for *stark*, *name in the of God* for *in the name of God*, *cowsheds* for *cowsherds*, *cowherd* for *coward*, *trunchman* for *truchman*, *bfit* for *but*, *tist* for *'tis*, *fures* for *furies*, *hotiy* for *hotly rfist* for *first*, *tender* for *tinder*, Αυκχανου δε, παντος for Ἀμήχανον δὲ παντός, etc., etc. The editor more than once takes credit to himself for having 'followed the original word for word, and letter by letter with religious exactness, except in the case of a misplaced or inverted letter or some obvious clerical slip which it would have been absurd to perpetuate': I cannot therefore see upon what principle such instances as I have quoted were allowed to stand uncorrected.

Monsieur D'Olive, vol. i. p. 212 :—

'As private as I had King *Giris* Ring.'

Read, *Gyges*'.

Monsieur D'Olive, vol. i. p. 220 :—

'For how can you be ever sound or safe,
Where in so many red *steps* of your wounds
Gaspe in your eyes? with change of place be sure,
Like sicke men mending, you shall find recure.'

Read, *lips*, and perhaps *gape* for *gaspe* : Vandome

is speaking of St. Anne's dead wife, whose body he persists in keeping unburied ; and the sense is of course ' by doing which you give your wounds no chance of healing.'

Monsieur D'Olive, vol. i. p. 235 :—

' I did ever dreame, that this head was borne to bear a *breadth*, this shoulder to support a state, this face to looke bigg, this bodie to beare a presence, these feete were borne to be reuellers, and these calues were borne to be courtiers : In a worde, I was borne Noble, and I will die Noblie.'

Read, ' to bear a *brain.*'

The Gentleman Usher, vol. i. p. 258 :—

'Or (to say true) *nay of* honest part.'

Read, *of any.*

The Gentleman Usher, vol. i. p. 267 :—

' Bright Nimph, that Boare figured your crueltie
Chared by love, defended by your beautie.'

Read, *Chasèd.*

The Gentleman Usher, vol. i. p. 268 :—

' O, my lord Medice became it rarely,
Me thought I likde his manly being *out*
It becomes Noblemen to doe nothing *well.*'

Transpose *out* and *well.*

The Gentleman Usher, vol. i. p. 283 :—

' O these be *godly* gudgeons : *where's the deedes*
The perfect Nobleman ? '

Read,

' O, these be *goodly* gudgeons, *whereas the deed's*
The perfect nobleman.'

The Gentleman Usher, vol. i. p. 315 :—

> 'No ladie, not a whit,
> *Stood*, and you think to make an Asse of me,
> May chance to rise betimes ; I know't, I know.'

A line seems to be missing after *me*, and of course *stood* should be *'sblood*.

The Gentleman Usher, vol. i. p. 538 :—

> 'Hence haplesse Ornaments that adorn'd his head :
> Disorder ever these *entering carles*
> And leave my beautie like a wildernesse.'

Read, *enticing curls*.

Bussy d'Ambois, vol. ii. p. 10 :—

> 'And because
> His Grace's pleasure is to give your good
> His Passe through my Command : Me thinks you might
> Use me with more respect.'

After *good*, *lordship* seems to have dropped out; and there should be only a comma after *command*.

Bussy d'Ambois, vol. ii. p. 59 :—

> 'That y' aue a tongue so scandalous, 'twill cut
> A perfect crystall ; and a breath that will
> Kill *to that wall* a spider.'

Qy.

> 'That you've a tongue so scandalous, 'twill cut
> A perfect crystal ; and a breath that will
> Kill *equal to* a spider?'

Bussy d'Ambois, vol. ii. p. 82 :—

> 'So nature laies
> A deal of stuffe together, and by use,
> Or by the mere necessitie of matter,
> Ends such a worke, fils it, or leaues it emptie,
> Of strength, or vertue, error or deere truth ;
> Not knowing what she does ; but usually
> Gives that which she calls merit to a man,
> And *beliefe must arriue* him on huge riches,
> Honour, and happinesse, that effects his ruine ;
> Even as in ships of warre, whose lasts of powder
> Are laid (men think) to make them *last, and guards,*
> When a disorder'd sparke that powder taking,
> Blowes up with sudden violence and horror
> Ships that kept emptie, had sail'd long with terror.'

Here the line 'And beliefe ... riches' seems to me manifestly corrupt. Even if the construction 'arrive him on huge riches' is allowable, it is obvious that *belief* alone would not produce such a result, still less would it be a *necessary* consequence. I would read,

> 'And *he lief* must *arride* him on huge riches,'

i.e. and he cannot help pleasing himself with the certainty of huge riches, as a consequence of his merit. For *last, and guards,* I propose *lasting guards*.

The Revenge of Bussy d'Ambois, vol. ii. p. 108:—

> 'As twere *not all,*
> Or made by custom nothing.'

Read, *not at all.*

The Revenge of Bussy d'Ambois, vol. ii. p. 113:—

> 'The *splenative* Philosopher that ever
> Laught at them all,' etc.

Read, *splenativ'st*.

The Revenge of Bussy d'Ambois, vol. ii. p. 134:—

> 'So great in Athens grew, that *he* erected
> Three hundred statues of him.'

Read, *she*, *i.e.* Athens.

The Revenge of Bussy d'Ambois, vol. ii. p. 143:—

> 'Good and bad hold neuer
> Any thing common: you can neuer finde
> Things *outward care*, but you neglect your minde.
> God hath the whole worlde perfect made and free;
> His parts to the vse of th' all; men then that *are*
> Parts of that all, must as the general sway
> Of that importeth, willingly obay,' etc.

I would read, 'Things outward *worth* care;' and *be* for *are*, the passage from this point being all rhymed verse.

Byrons Conspiracie, Prologue, vol. ii. p. 186:—

> 'As when in wealthy Autumne, his bright starre
> (Washt in the lofty Ocean) thence ariseth;
> Illustrates heaven, and all his other fires
> Outshines and darkens: so admird Byron,
> All France exempted from comparison,
> He toucht heaven with his lance; nor yet was toucht
> With hellish treacherie: his countries love,
> He yet thirsts: not the *faire shades* of himselfe:
> Of which empoisoned Spring; when policie drinkes,
> He bursts in growing great; and rising, sinckes.'

Read,
> 'his country's love
> He yet thirsts, not the *fierce hates* of himself;'

i.e. not for the gratification of his own fierce hatred against his country. For *thirsts*, used transitively, compare *Cæsar and Pompey*, vol. iii. p. 158, 'Who more *thirsts* the conquest than resolves to bear the foil.'

Byrons Conspiracie, vol. ii. p. 211 :—

> 'Against two squadrons, *but with* fifty horse.'

Probably transpose *but* and *with*.

Byrons Conspiracie, vol. ii. p. 223 :—

> 'And as a glorious Poeme fronted well
> With many a goodly herald of his praise,
> So farre from hate of praises to his face,
> That he praies men to praise him, and they ride
> Before, with trumpets in their mouthes, proclayming
> Life to the holie furie of his lines:
> All drawne, as if with one eye he had leerd,
> On his lou'd hand, and led it by a rule;
> That his plumes only imp the muses wings,
> He sleepes with them, his head is napt with baies,
> His lips break out with Nectar, his tunde feet
> Are of the great *last*, the perpetual motion,
> And he puft *wirh* their empty breath beleeues
> Full merit, *eas'd*, those passions of winde,
> Which yet serue, but to praise, and cannot merit,
> And so his furie in their ayre expires.'

Read, I think,

> 'His lips break out with nectar, his tuned feet
> Are of the great *blast* the perpetual motion,

> And he, puffed *with* their empty breath, believes
> Full merit *caused* those passions of wind,
> Which yet serve but to praise,' etc.

The whole passage is villainously punctuated as usual.

Byrons Conspiracie, vol. ii. p. 241 :—

> 'Drowne the *dead* noises of my sword in laughter.'

Read, *dread*.

Byrons Conspiracie, vol. ii. p. 254 :—

> 'When guilty, *made* Noblesse, feed on Noblesse.'

Read,

> 'When guilty, *mad* Noblesse *fed* on Noblesse.'

Byrons Conspiracie, vol. ii. p. 255 :—

> 'Let him by vertue, quite *out of* from fortune,
> Her fetterd shoulders, and her winged shoes.'

Read,

> 'Let him by virtue quite *cut off* from fortune,' etc.

Compare *Cæsar and Pompey*, vol. iii. p. 155, 'so may fortune now, displume her shoulders, cast off her wing'd shooes.'

Byrons Tragedie, vol. ii. p. 256 :—

> 'To your unmatcht, and more than humaine *winde*.'

Read, *mind*.

Byrons Tragedie, vol ii. p. 282 :—

> 'Noble happy beast,
> That *hie*, not having to their wills to live.'

Read, *die*.

Byrons Tragedie, vol. ii. p. 285 :—

'The Duke instructs me
With such grave lessons of *mortallitie*.'

Read, *morality*.

Byrons Tragedie, vol. ii. p. 288 :—

'All this my Lord to me is *misery*.'

Read, *mystery*.

Byrons Tragedie, vol. ii. p. 292 :—

'All popular gifts,
Are coullors, *it* will bear no vineger.'

Read,

'Are colours *that* will bear,' etc.

Byrons Tragedie, vol. ii. p. 296 :—

'Assaults the light, strikes down himself, not *out*.'

Read, *it*.

Byrons Tragedie, vol. ii. p. 304 :—

'The vengeful *Saturnals* of the league.'

Read, ' *Saturnalians* of the league.'

Byrons Tragedie, vol. ii. p. 306 :—

'*Though* we may condole.'

Read, *although*.

Byrons Tragedie, vol. ii. p. 307 :—

'The clowdes (obseruing their Aeriall natures)
Are borne aloft, and then to moisture *hang'd*'

Read, *chang'd*.

Byrons Tragedie, vol. ii. p. 312 :—

'(Being but one man) *render* the kingdomes dome.'

Read, *under*.

Byrons Tragedie, vol. ii. p. 314 :—

' I know this bodie but a sinck of folly,
The groundwork, and rais'd frame of woe and frailtie :
The bond and bundle of corruption ;
A quick corse, onely sensible of griefe,
A walking sepulcher, or household thiefe :
A glasse of ayre, broken with lesse than breath,
A slaue bound face to face, to death, till death :
And what *sayd* all you more ? I know, besides
That life is but a darke and stormy night,
Of sencelesse dreams, terrors, and broken sleepes ;
A Tyrannie, deuising paines to plague
And make man long in dying, racks his death ;
And death is nothing ; what can you say more ?
I *bring a long* globe, *and* a little *earth*,
Am seated like earth betwixt both the heauens :
That if I rise ; to heauen I rise ; if fall
I likewise fall to heauen ; what stronger faith,
Hath any of your soules ? what say you more ? '

Read,

' I *being* a *blown* globe *of* a little *breath* ';

comparing a few lines above ' A glasse of ayre broken with lesse than breath ' ; in the next line but one to which *sayd* should be *say*.

Byrons Tragedie, vol. ii. p. 314 :—

' When I have lost my armes, my fame, my *winde*.'

Read, *mind*.

Byrons Tragedie, vol. ii. p. 318 :—

'Thou seest I see not? yet *I* speake as I saw.'

Qy. *you* ?

May-Day, vol. ii. p. 335 :—

'. . . for your place, take it as it fals, but so as you thinke no place *to* good for you ; fall *too with* ceremony whatsoeuer the company be.'

Read, *too*, and ' fall *to with* ceremony,' etc.

May-Day, vol. ii. p. 347 :—

'Crownes, *chickins*, bracelets.'

Read, *chequins*.

May-Day, vol. ii. p. 366 :—

'Now your worship is Oracle to your owne miracles ; how you shine in this smoaky cloud? which you make the golden net to embrace Venus, y 'aue past the pikes yfaith, and all the *Iayles* of the love-god swarme in yonder house, to salute your recovery.'

Read, *joys*.

May-Day, vol. ii. p. 371 :—

'But indeed I thinke it safer to sit closer, and so to cloud the *summe* of my visnomy, that no eye discerne it.'

Read, *sun*.

May-Day, vol. ii. p. 376 :—

'And therefore, though I held it good discretion in me to winke at the blow not *seeing* to take notice of it.'

Read, *seeming*.

May-Day, vol. ii. p. 379 :—

'I tell thee I smelt a voice here in my entry, s'fut he make it smell worse *and' cheare* it againe.'

What is the point in making Quintilliano speak broad Somersetshire here? Why not, 'and I hear it,' *i.e.* if I hear it?

May-Day, vol. ii. p. 384 :—

> '*In the more then* temper my late rage
> And show *your* vertues perfectly deriued
> From the Venetian noblesse.'

Read,

> '*I'll do thee more than* temper my late rage,
> And show *you* virtues,' etc.

A few lines above, for *remnine* read *remain*, and for *miads* read *minds*.

May-Day, vol. ii. p. 385 :—

> 'In any honoured *vse shall* command.'

Read,

> 'In any honour'd use *you* shall command.'

May-Day, vol. ii. p. 386 :—

> 'A poxe upon thee, tame your bald *hewed* tougne.'

Read, *bald-haired*.

The Widdowes Teares, vol. iii. p. 48 :—

'Cry mercie Sir, here's a whole chorus of Syluans at hand, *cornetting*, and tripping ath' toe,' etc.

Qy. *curvetting*?

The Widdowes Teares, vol. iii. p. 55 :—

' If the braine of the *West* were in the heades of the learned ; then might Parish-Clerkes be common counsaile men.'

Read, *wise*.

The Widdowes Teares, vol. iii. p. 69 :—

' *Canero.* What ? thy husbands bodie ? '

Read, *Cancro* : see Florio, *Italian Dictionary* : ' *Cáncaro, Cánchero, Cáncro*, one of the twelve signs in the Zodiacke, called Cancer ; also the Crab-star ; also any sea-crab ; also that foul, devouring sore or evil, called a Canker, *much used among the Italians for a bitter curse, one to another*, as we use to wish *the pox to our enemies ; used also for an interjection of denial or refusal*.'

The Widdowes Teares, vol. iii. p. 70 :—

' Let me be brought
To die for that most famous villanie ;
Not for this miching base transgression
Of *tenant* negligence.'

Read, *truant*.

The Widdowes Teares, vol. iii. p. 71 :—

' Thou foolish thirster after idle secrets, And ill's abrode ; looke horne, and *store* and choke thee ;
There sticks an *Achelons* horne of *all*, Copie enough.
As much as Alizon of streames receiues,
Or loftie *Ilea* showes of shadie leaues.'

On this passage the editor has the following

note: 'The first line [*i.e.* There sticks ... enough] seems hopelessly corrupt. I once thought the words "Copie enough" were attributable rather to the printer's devil than to Lysander, and had got interpolated into the text through the stupidity of the compositor and the negligence of the "reader." But I find that a former editor of this play explains "Copie" as *Copia*, and supposes the passage to refer to the cornucopia, or horn of plenty.'

The reference in *Achelons* [*i.e. Achelous'*] *horne* is of course to the cornucopia, but 'Copie enough' is equally of course merely a marginal *explanation* of those words. Read,

> 'Thou foolish thirster after idle secrets,
> And [*i.e.* if] ill's abroad, look *home*, and *stare* and choke thee;
> There sticks an *Achelous'* horn of *ill*,
> As much as Alison of streams receives,
> Or lofty *Ida* shows of shady leaves.'

The Widdowes Teares, vol. iii. p. 82:—

> 'If you *Parrat* to me long; goe to.'

Read, *prate*.

Cæsar and Pompey, vol. iii. p. 136:—

> 'And where all fortune is renounc't, no reason
> Will think one man *transfer'd* with affectation
> Of all Romes Empire.'

Qy. *transformed* or *transfused*?

Cæsar and Pompey, vol. iii. p. 152 :—

> '. . . . but I doubt
> There will come humble offer on his part,
> Of honor'd peace to you, for whose sweet name
> So cryed out to you in our late-met Senate
> *Lost* no fit offer of that wished treaty.'

Read, *Lose.*

Cæsar and Pompey, vol. iii. p. 155 :—

> 'O night, O jealous night, of all the noblest
> Beauties, and glories, where the gods have stroke
> There *foure* digestions, from thy gastly chaos,
> Blush thus to drowne them all in this houre sign'd
> By the necessity of fate for Cæsar.'

That *foure* should be *sour* is evident, but *stroke* also looks to me corrupt. A few lines above *Ram* should be *ram.*

Cæsar and Pompey, vol iii. p. 167 :—

> 'I beare the touch of feare for all their safeties,
> *Or* for mine owne? *enlarge* with twice as many
> Selfe-liues, selfe-fortunes? they shall sink beneath
> Their own credulities, before I crosse them.'

Read and punctuate as follows :—

> 'I bear the touch of fear for all their safeties,
> *Not* for mine own : *enlarged* with twice as many
> Self-lives, self-fortunes, they shall sink beneath,' etc.

Cæsar and Pompey, vol. iii. p. 168 :—

> 'Inscrib'd with this true *soull* of funerall.'

Read, *scroll.*

Cæsar and Pompey, vol. iii. p. 171 :—

> 'Cato sole *accepted*.'

Read, *excepted*.

Cæsar and Pompey, vol. iii. p. 171 :—

> 'Come Demetrius,
> We now must sute our habites to our fortunes.'
> And since these changes ever change to greatest

Transpose the two last lines.

Cæsar and Pompey, vol. iii. p. 174 :—

> '*Tongue, shew*, falsehood, are
> *To* bloodiest deaths his parts so much admir'd,
> Vaine glory, villany.'

Qy.

> '*Tongue-show*, falsehood, are
> *The* bloodiest deaths ; his parts,' etc. ?

Alphonsus, vol. iii. p. 218 :—

> '*Empress*. Nephew, she thinks you mock her in *her* mirth.
> *Edward*. I think the Princes make a scorn of me.
> If any do, I'l prove it with my sword,
> That English courtship *leaves* it from the world.'

Read, *your*, and *braves*.

Revenge for Honour, vol. iii. p. 290 :—

> '*ancouge* the 12 signs.'

Read, *among*.

Revenge for Honour, vol. iii. p. 293 :—

> 'I cannot play the fool rightly, I mean, the Physician
> Without I have licence to *expalcat*
> On the disease.'

Read, *expatiate*.

Revenge for Hononr. vol. iii. p. 301 :—

'. . . . . doubt not
That I 'll *deceive* your trust.'

Read, *deserve*.

Revenge for Honour, vol. iii. p. 317 :—

'To me
. .*Count* that cure, I 'll stand between the Lady
And Mura's fury.'

Read, *commit*.

HEYWOOD[1]

Edward IV. vol. i. p. 83 :—

> 'Ah, Jane, this kills my heart,
> That thou reckes others, and not *rust* my smart.

Read, *ru'st*, *i.e.* ruest.

I. *Edward IV.* vol. i. p. 105 :—

> 'By blazing to the world his high deserts
> Of wisedom, valour, and *his* heroicke birth?'

Omit *his*, caught from the line above.

II. *Edward IV.* vol. i. p. 119 :—

> 'You must imagine since you saw him last
> Preparde for trauaile, he hath been abroade,
> And seene the sundry fashions of the world,
> Vlysses-like, his countries loue at length,
> Hoping his wiues death, and to see his friends,
> Such as did sorrow for his great mishaps,
> Come home is hee ; but so unluckily
> As he is like to loose his life thereby.'

There seems to be a confusion of constructions here between 'his country's love and the hope of finding his wife dead have brought him home,' and 'through love of his country and hope of his wife's death, he is come home.'

[1] The references are to Pearson's Reprint, 6 vols. 1874.

II. *Edward IV.* vol. i. p. 156:—

'I warrant you, woman, be not so afraid.
If not this bloud-stone hang'd about his necke,
This balme will stanch it, by the helpe of God.
Lift vp his arme, whilst I do bathe his wound.
The *sign* belike was here *when* he was hurt,
Or else some principal and chief vein is pierst.'

I think we should read,

'The *sinew* belike was here *where* he was hurt.'

The anatomical knowledge of our old dramatists seems to have been very vague: thus, in *Hamlet*, i. 4. 82, 83,

'My fate cries out,
And makes each petty artery in this body
As hardy as the Nemean's lion's nerve,'

Shakespeare apparently looks upon arteries and nerves as being of the same texture; and Heywood may have supposed that sinews bled when severed. In *The Faithful Friends*, iii. 3. p. 264, ed. Dyce, there is perhaps the same vagueness of knowledge in the words:—

'Till my veins
And sinews crack, I'll stretch my utmost strength.'

II. *Edward IV.* vol. i. p. 160:—

'So you did swear you would be true to Shore;
But you were not so good as your word.
My *oathes disherit which* by the King's command.'

Qy.,

'My *oath's disherited* by the King's command'?

i.e. she is discharged of her vow to treat Jane with

Conjectural Readings 147

compassion by the king's command that no one should harbour or help her (Jane).

II. *Edward IV.* vol. i. p. 166 :—

> 'No man can say that he is master now
> Of anything is his, such is the tide
> Of *short* disturbance running through the land.'

Qy. *swift?*

I. *If you Know not Me*, etc., vol. i. p. 197 :—

> 'If your highness will
> Your own estate preserue, you must foresee
> *Fore* danger,' etc.

Read, *Your*; *Fore* having been caught from *foresee.*

I. *If you Know not Me*, etc., vol. i. p. 239 :—

> 'For there's another raised, more base than he,
> Poole, that *Arch, for* truth and honesty.'

Read,

> 'Poole, that *arch-foe* to truth and honesty.'

I. *If you Know not Me*, etc., vol. i. p. 245 :—

> 'Be not ashamed, man; look me in the face.
> Who have you now to *patronize* your strictness on.'

Qy., *practise?*

II. *If you Know not Me*, etc., vol. i. p. 270 :—

'I must tell you John, and I know it, you have not fed of the spirituall food, *but edified* by faithe and *suffered* the tares of the wild affections to be burnt.'

Read, 'but *be* edified by faith and *suffer,*' etc.

II. *If you Know not Me*, etc., vol. i. p. 307 :—

> 'I have tride ere now
> The sweaty Spaniard, and the carowsing Dane,
> The foggy Dutchman, and the fiery French,
> The briske Italian, and indeed what not;
> And yet of all and all, the Englishman
> Shall goe for me: I, y'are the truest louers,
> The ablest, *last night*, and the truest men
> That breathe beneath the sun.'

Qy. *lastingest*? The *n* and *i* being transposed, the change of *est* to *ht* would naturally follow. In the same line *truest* has probably been caught from the one above.

The Faire Maide of the Exchange, vol. ii. p. 40 :—

> 'Speake, why *then* I say?'

Read, 'why *when*? I say.'

The Faire Maide of the Exchange, vol. ii. p. 40 :—

> 'I know your wifulnesse,
> These words are but to show the world your humour:
> I often use to square these parchment pieces
> Without occasion: I'm sure you are not writing,
> The Lawnes you late bought,' etc.

Punctuate,

> 'I often use to square these parchment pieces:
> Without occasion I'm sure you are not writing.
> The lawns,' etc.

i.e. You have other business in hand, and I am sure you never write unless you are obliged, and therefore you cannot have need of these sheets of parchment.

The Faire Maide of the Exchange, vol. ii. p. 47 :—

'I could doe more, for I could make enquiry
Where the best-witted gallants use to dine

. . . . . .

And over-heare their talke, observe their humours,
Collect their jeasts, put them into play,
And *tire* them too with payment to behold
What I have filcht from them.'

Read either *lure* or *tice*.

The Faire Maide of the Exchange, vol. ii. p. 64 :—

'I will resigne the same
To you my friend, knowing my unworthy selfe
Too foule for such a beauty and too base
To match in brightnesse with that sacred comet
That shines like Phœbus in *London's* element.'

Read, *Love's*.

The Faire Maide of the Exchange, vol. ii. p. 69 :—

'What are you cursing too? then we catch no fish :
Comes there any more, here's two *Snights* to a dish.'

Mr. Barron Field reads *knights*, which seems meaningless. I believe *snights* is sound, it being merely another spelling of *snite, i.e.* snipe, a word used like 'woodcock' for a fool, empty-headed fellow; the snights here being Frank's two brothers, whom he has gulled about Phillis. Lydgate, *apud* Halliwell, *Dictionary of Archaic and Provincial Words*, has 'A downg-hille doke as deynté as a *snyghte*.'

The Faire Maide of the Exchange, vol. ii. p. 78 :—

'You love my daughter ; so *you thought* you said ;
You said moreover that she loves you well.'

Read, *methought.*

A Woman Kild with Kindnes, vol. ii. p. 99 :—

'I but our Merlin first had plum'd the Fowle,
And twice *renew'd* her from the River too.'

Read, *enew'd.* A writer in the *Edinburgh Review,* for October 1872, has shown that this word was a term in common use in aquatic falconry. 'If the fowl succeeded in swerving towards the water, she escaped with comparative immunity. In this case the hawk might stoop and sometimes apparently even strike without doing much damage, as the blow could not be followed up, the fowl taking refuge in diving. In this case the fowl was said to be *enewed*—the hawk *enewed* the fowl; that is, forced it back to the water again, from which it had to be driven afresh by the falconer, and landed before the hawk could stoop and seize, or strike and truss her quarry. The fowl was often enewed once or twice before it was landed effectively enough for the final swoop. From this explanation of its meaning the etymology of enew will be apparent; and in support of it we have in Kelham's *Norman Dictionary* ' *Enewance de draps,* watering of cloth '; while Cotgrave gives *eneaüer,* 'to turn into water,' and *eneaüe,* 'watered, turned into water.' The

Reviewer then quotes passages from Drayton and Turberville illustrating the use of the term; other instances will be found in Murray's *English Dictionary*.

A Woman Kild with Kindnes, vol. ii. p. 111:—

'Such is my fate, to this *suite* was I borne,
 To wear rich pleasures crowne, or fortunes scorne.'

Qy. repeat *fate* for *suite*?

A Woman Kild with Kindnes, vol. ii. p. 115:—

'Rac'd from the *bed*-roll of Gentility.'

Read, '*bead*-roll'; and after 'glow'd within,' three lines lower, put a colon.

A Woman Kild with Kindnes, vol. ii. p. 121:—

'Before the double guilt, the *well-hatch* Ore,' etc.

Read, *well-hatch'd*.

The Foure Prentises of London, vol. ii. p. 219:—

'Shall our *bar'd* horses clime yond Mountain tops.'

Read *bard*. The word has nothing to do with the verb to *bare*, but is from the French *bardé*, 'which,' says the Edinburgh Reviewer quoted above, 'Cotgrave renders "barbed, or trapped like a great horse."'

The Foure Prentises of London, vol. ii. p. 251:—

'Tancred behold the Lady you once *ceas'd*.'

Read, *seized*—a very common misspelling.

The Faire Maid of the West, vol. ii. p. 287 :—

'Sir will you *take* the wine.'

Read, *taste*; see quotation from *The Silver Age*, vol. iii. p. 100, given below, and note on *The Insatiate Countess*, iii. 4. 96.

The Faire Maid of the West, vol. ii. p. 384 :—

'I could be angry with you above measure,
In *your* four deaths I die, that had before
Tasted but one.'

Read, *you*.

The Faire Maid of the West, vol. ii. p. 389 :—

'And by the devils first spew'd *upon* earth.'

Read, *up on*.

The Golden Age, vol. iii. p. 26 :—

'Should all affect the strict life you desire,
The world it selfe would end when we expire,
Posterity is *all, heavens* number fill,
Which by your helpe may be increased still.'

Qy. 'posterity is all heaven's number fill'? with the sense that it is posterity alone that helps to fill up the number of heaven.

The Golden Age, vol. iii. p. 40 :—

'Here *ease* my life, for them thou shalt not kill.'

Qy. *cease*?

The Golden Age, vol. iii. p. 68 :—

> 'Charming sleepe
> Deaths yonger brother, show thyself as *still lesse*
> As death himself.'

Read, *stir-less*.

The Golden Age, vol. iii. p. 69 :—

> They are deafe in rest; then gentle sweet *ly* further,
> If you should call, I thus your voyce would murther,
> And strangle with my kisses.'

Can *ly* be sound, or should we read, '*no* further'?

The Siluer Age, vol. iii. p. 91 :—

> 'The keene-edged *harpe*.'

It would be better to print *harpé* or *Harpé*, the well-known scimitar of Perseus.

The Siluer Age, vol. iii. p. 100 :—

> ' Whose powerful arme gaue strength unto my Lord
> To *worste* his safety through these dangerous warres.'

Read, *work*.

The Siluer Age, vol. iii. p. 159 :—

> '*Danae* spare your tubs.'

Read, *Danaids*.

The Brazen Age, vol. iii. p. 174 :—

> 'Nere let my streames wash Acarnania's bankes
> Or *we* confin'de in Thoas.'

Read, *be*.

The Brazen Age, vol. iii. p. 196 :—

'And but *an* equall language.'

Read, *on*.

The Brazen Age, vol. iii. p. 235 :—

'If I can catch them, all the Gods I'll call
To see my wrongs, their sports I'll neere *to marre*,
And venge me on that letcherous God of warre.'

Qy. *to-mar*, *i.e.* thoroughly to mar?

The Brazen Age, vol. iii. p. 249 :—

'Shall torture pale our cheeke? No, Priest proceed,
We will not feele the paine, thou shalt not *breed*.'

Qy. *brede*, *i.e.* burn? Hercules is in his death-agony from the poisoned shirt. A little lower down for 'my bulk *in flames*,' read *inflames*.

1. *The Iron Age*, vol. iii. p. 273 :—

'The *Chritian* scepter now in contrauersie.'

Read, *Cretan*.

1. *The Iron Age*, vol. iii. p. 288 :—

'*Faire* Heauen I doe.'

Read, *Fore*.

1. *The Iron Age*, vol. iii. p. 304 :—

'And *weare* it Diomed.'

Read, *swear*.

1. *The Iron Age*, vol. iii. p. 309 :—

'Yet shall no stroke fall from Achilles arme
Faire Polixena, so powerful is thy charme.'

Qy. omit *Faire*?

Conjectural Readings

1. *The Iron Age*, vol. iii. p. 313 :—

'Had I lost a Patroclus, a deere friend
  As thou hast done, I would have dond these armes
  In which he dyed, sprung through the Troian hoast,
  And mauger opposition, *let the blow*
  Or by the same hand dy'd.'

Read, *laid them low.*

1. *The Iron Age*, vol. iii. p. 331 :—

'*Though* the dammage you have done to Troy,
  Might *cease* our armes, and arme our browes with wrath,' etc.

Read, *although*; but what does '*cease* our armes' mean? Can it mean put a stop to the embraces they had just interchanged?

1. *The Iron Age*, vol. iii. p. 333 :—

'How cheeres Achilles, though thy too much pride
  Which held the heart of Ajax from thy loue,
  He'll be the formost to reuenge thy death.'

Read, *Withheld*, and put a note of interrogation after 'Achilles.' A few lines lower down for 'send *to* youthfull Pirhus,' read 'send *the*,' etc.

1. *The Iron Age*, vol. iii. p. 337 :—

'Thou that fightst all *byd* craft *an* in the night.'

Read, '*by* craft *and* in,' etc.

1. *The Iron Age*, vol. iii. p. 339 :—

'He had a Bow too *much* Achilles drew,
  So by his strength the Ithacan him knew.'

Read,
  'He had a bow, too, *which*,' etc.

I. *The Iron Age*, vol. iii. p. 345 :—

'Hector, a *worthy Call*,' etc.

Read,

'Hector, a *Worthy call'd*,' etc.

Hector being the first of the three Gentile Worthies.

II. *The Iron Age*, vol. iii. p. 368 :—

'Penthesilea, with her *bustain* troopes.'

Read, *buskin'd*.

II. *The Iron Age*, vol. iii. p. 370 :—

'If then a villaine
Can driue into their eares, the goddesse Pallas
Offended for the stolne Palladium :
(*Will* you erect this Machine to her honour?)
Withall that it were brought into her Temple,' etc.

Read, *will'd* (*i.e.* desired), putting commas after 'Pallas,' 'Palladium,' and 'honour,' and removing the brackets.

II. *The Iron Age*, vol. iii. p. 406 :—

Pyr. Beauteous Lady,
The great'st ambition Pyrhus aymes at now,
Is how to know you farther.
Her. . . . .
Hath been so mighty to revenge the wrongs
Of my faire mother, can from Hermione
Challenge no lesse than welcome.'

I would insert for the missing words 'The hero who.'

Conjectural Readings. 157

II. *The Iron Age*, vol. iii. p. 409 :—

'Oh Cethus, what's this musicke vnto me,
That am compos'd of discords? what are healths
To him that is struck heart-sicke? all those joyes
Whose *leaders* seem to pierce *against* the roofes
Of these high structures, to him that is struck downe
Half way below the Center?'

Qy. 'Whose *peal does* seem to pierce *again* the roofs,' etc. ?

II. *The Iron Age*, vol. iii. p. 420 :—

'*And* undertake that one man easily spar'd,' etc.

Read, *But*.

The English Traveller, vol. iv. p. 16 :—

'*Rob*. Farewell Musk-cat.
Reig. Adue good Cheese and Oynons, stuff thy guts
With *Specke* and Barley-pudding for disgestion.'

Read, *spelt*, *i.e.* vetches.

The English Traveller, vol. iv. p. 22 :—

'To preuent Surfit
Thy Diet, shall bee to one Dish confin'd
And that too *Rifled*, with as vncleane hands,
As ere were laid on thee.'

Qy. *rosted*, *i.e.* roasted ?

The English Traveller, vol. iv. pp. 26, 27 :—

'Enough, enough, your wit hath plai'd too long upon
    our patience ;
Wife, it grieues me much both for the yong and old
    man, the one

> Graces his head with care, endures the parching heat,
> and biting cold,
> The terrours of the Lands, and feares at Sea in trauel,
> onely to gaine
> Some competent estate to leaue his sonne.'

Divide the lines at 'long' ... 'much' ... 'Graces' ... 'heat' ... 'Lands' ... 'gaine,' and for *Lands* read *land*.

The English Traveller, vol. iv. p. 73 :—

> 'Well, if he now come off well, Fox you all;
> Goe, call for wine.'

Qy. 'Well, if he now come; off! well fox you all'? *i.e.* make yourselves well drunk.

The English Traveller, vol. iv. p. 87 :—

> 'But though their riots tript *at* my estate.'

Read, *up*.

A Mayden-head well Lost, vol. iv. p. 110 :—

> 'To hast your marriage with the *former* Prince.'

Read, *Parma*.

A Mayden-head well Lost, vol. iv. p. 127 :—

> 'Come Mounsieur, night steales on, not many *yeares*
> Shall passe me,' etc.

Read, *hours*; and so again p. 129 for 'some two *yeares* after.'

A Mayden-head well Lost, vol. iv. p. 128 :—

> 'Nor adde vnto your blushes by *our rude* reproofes.'

Qy. omit *our rude*?

Conjectural Readings

A Mayden-head well Lost, vol. iv. p. 130:—

'Goodly large Arras . . . he hath caus'd to be hang'd round about the Chamber: My Lady and Mistresse, now my Lady,' etc.

Read, 'the chamber *of* my Lady and Mistress; now my Lady,' etc.

A Mayden-head well Lost, vol. iv. p. 146:—

'That *youd* be a Mecenas unto virtue.'

Read, *would*.

A Mayden-head well Lost, vol. iv. p. 156:—

'Come Mounsieur, now 'tis cast,
Reuenge neere *rules*, so it be found at last.'

Read, *rues*.

A Mayden-head well Lost, vol. iv. p. 164:—

'You crowne me with *your* wishes, Royall father.'

Read, *my*.

The Witches of Lancashire, vol. iv. p. 178:—

'Your *monies* ready.'

Read, *money's*.

The Witches of Lancashire, vol. iv. p. 181:—

'Why . . . you may look *of out*.'

Read *off on't*; and a few lines below for 'But this time forget,' read, 'But *for* this time,' etc.

The Witches of Lancashire, vol. iv. p. 182:—

'Give me a *stroke* and Ile beat him.'

Qy. *stick*?

The Witches of Lancashire, vol. iv. p. 189 :—

   ' I shall know thee *Peg*, by thy grissel'd *gut*.'

Qy. *Meg*, and *scut* ?

The Witches of Lancashire, vol. iv. p. 191 :—

   ' We'l try if we can finde in our way home
   When Hares come from their coverts, to *reliffe*,
   A course or two.'

I can make nothing of *reliffe*, unless it should be *relieve*, *i.e. alvum exonerare*. With rabbits it is a habit to seek a spot for this purpose away from their burrows ; but hares do not burrow (at all events in England), and I am not aware of their having this habit.

The Witches of Lancashire, vol. iv. p. 196 :—

   ' Give me the keies, ile stand *it all* danger.

Read, ' stand it *at* all danger.'

The Witches of Lancashire, vol. iv. p. 199 :—

' There will I tie you, . . . and though not *lash* you, yet ash you whilest my switch will hold.'

Read, *leash*.

The Witches of Lancashire, vol. iv. p. 207 :—

   ' Sir I will not goe about to over-rule your reason, bu
      for my part
   I will not out of a house on a Bridall day, till I see the
      last man borne.'

After *borne* add *out*.

A Challenge for Beauty, vol. v. p. 9 :—

> '*Nay*, we terme this law,
> Or meere oppression.'

Read,

> '*May* we term this law,
> Or mere oppression?'

A Challenge for Beauty, vol. v. p. 12 :—

'*Ald.* Ene in the mid'st meane, daughter, or let me see and thou wilt be ruld by me, beare thyself—E'ne how thou wilt, provided it be to thine own profit, and my further honour: Noble Bonavide *has Valladaur a daughter?* do you know this gallant.

'*Petr. Valladaura I hate*, this gentleman acquainted with my beauty, reveald it to Bonavide: Sir you haue bound me to you, and comes to usher him to my presence.'

The text as it stands is nonsense. Read,

'*Ald.* E'en in the midst mean, daughter, or, let me see, and [*i.e.* an] thou wilt be ruled by me, bear thyself—e'en how thou wilt, provided it be to thine own profit, and my further honour. Noble Bonavide—*ha!* [*Enter Valladaura*] daughter, do you know this gallant?

'*Petr. Valladaura! I ha't* [*i.e.* I have it, understand the meaning of matters], this gentleman, acquainted with my beauty, revealed it to Bonavide,—Sir, you have bound me to you,—and comes,' etc.

A Challenge for Beauty, vol. v. p. 13 :—

> ' I writ myselfe
> (And truly) lover ere I could write man,
> *Passing my service as a star*, where she
> The blest Idea of thy glorious feature,
> Drawn by the curious working of my thoughts
> Gave me *the* better,' etc.

Read, '*paying* my service as *to* a star,' and 'gave me *thee* better,' *i.e.* 'made you seem superior to any star.'

A Challenge to Beauty, vol. v. p. 17 :—

> ' For her breeding,
> It hath been 'mongst her equalls, and so farre
> From least taxation, to the *sayle* of tongues
> It merits imitation.'

Read, *soil*; omit the comma after 'taxation' and put one after 'tongues.'

A Challenge for Beauty, vol. v. p. 23 :—

' As of the man himself, *more* frivolous and idle.'

Read, *mere*.

A Challenge for Beauty, vol. v. p. 39 :—

' *Cent.* You find her pliant.
' *Pin.* As a thing of wax, never was thrifty trader more willing to put *of* a *sulke* commodity than she was to truck for her maydenhead.'

For *of*, of course read *off*; but is *sulke* genuine, or should we read *sullied*?

A Challenge for Beauty, vol. v. p. 47 :—

> ' What wilt thou *feele* me still ? '

Read, *fool*.

A Challenge for Beauty, vol. v. p. 48 :—

> ' I am shee.
> That beg to be *implyde* so.'

Read, *employed*, and remove the full stop after *shee*.

A Challenge for Beauty, vol. v. p. 59 :—

' Vnseene I left 'em, and by a private key,
  Went to my chamber, where I *said*, I 'll dare call her
  Neither my wife, nor Bride ; your lustfull daughter.'

Read,

' Unseen I left 'em, and by a private key
  Went to my chamber, where I *spied*—I 'll dare call her
  Neither my wife, nor bride.—your lustful daughter.'

A Challenge for Beauty, vol. v. p. 73 :—

        ' I am shee
For whom this noble Sir hath undertooke,
And wrongly stands convicted, this that body
So stain'd and sullied by these barbarous tongues,
That even in scolding *lies justice*, for heav'n
Hath forc't them to sweare truth.'

Perhaps we ought to read :—

'That even in *scolding justice lives*, for heaven,' etc.

But *scolding* looks to me questionable. A few lines above, after *calling* insert *is*, *i.e.* which is.

A Challenge for Beauty, vol. v. p. 77 :—

      ' You are shee
By whom I'll henceforth dress mee, and not weare
No hurt, of which you are not president.'

Read, *Honour* ; the *h* and *N* being transposed in printing.

Loues Mistris, vol. v. p. 98 :—

' If you meete Psiche, charge your Mercury
  To send *mee* to *her*.'

Transpose *mee* and *her*.

Loues Mistris, vol. v. p. 136 :—

   '*We shall* deceive the gods and goddesses,
    For a plow-jogging hinde.'

Transpose *wee* and *shall*, and put a note of interrogation after *hinde*.

Loues Mistriss, vol. v. p. 137 :—

      'This *cologing* wagge
       Will not be answered.'

Qy. *cogging*?

The Rape of Lucrece, vol. v. p. 246 :—

   'Weele prove *for Tarquin*, if they faile our hopes,
    Peace shall be made with Rome.'

Read, *our Tarquins*.

The Wise-woman of Hogsdon, vol. v. p. 281 :—

    'Nay M. Boyster,
   I barre you : let us work upon the winners.
   Gramercy *sinks*.'

Read, 'Gramercy, *cinques*.'

The Wise-woman of Hogsdon, vol. v. p. 319 :—

'I am satisfied good M. Harringsfield touching your friend, and since I see you have left his dangerous company, I *limit* you to bee a welcome guest unto my Table.'

Read, *invite*.

The Wise-woman of Hogsdon, vol. v. p. 330 :—

   'If he bee gone, then call mee *vent my griefe*,
    Father I am undone.'

Should we read *vent-my-grief* as one word

within inverted commas, and was there any flower popularly so called on the analogy of 'Love-in-idleness,' 'Heart's-ease,' 'Lady-smocks,' etc. ?

The Wise-woman of Hogsdon, vol. v. p. 333 :—

'If shee and you *see* me not, I am but dead.'

Qy. *save* ?

Procus and Puella, vol. vi. p. 120 :—

'Crookt-backt, *gow*-bellied, bending at the knee
His legs.'

Read, '*gor*-bellied'; and compare *i. H. iv.* ii. 2 93, 'Hang ye, *gor-bellied* knaves, are ye undone!'

Procus and Puella, vol. vi. p. 122 :—

'I had been in vaine ;
She onely *sties* to such as have no braine.'

Read, *flies.*

Earth and Age, vol. vi. p. 134 :—

'Let into Ganges *drops.*'

Read, *drop.*

Earth and Age, vol. vi. p. 138 :—

'Where's the Tarpeian masse, *sta ructure* none
More famous ?'

Read, *a structure.*

The Man-hater, vol. vi. p. 158 :—

'*Hie* expiat for
This inexhausted wickedness'

Read, *How.*

The Man-hater, vol. vi. p. 191 :—

'His guts full stuft, and braines well *toxt* with wine.'

Qy. *foxed?* Nares (*Glossary*) says, 'This word occurs twice in Heywood's *Philocothonista*, 1635, in the sense of *intoxicated*. We also find *toxing*, p. 29, intoxicating.' In all these cases I suspect there is the same misprint.

Jupiter and Io, vol. vi. p. 273 :—

"'Tis as I said before : but *having* her,
Some pretty tale, I prethee.'

Read, *leaving*.

Pelopœa and Alope, vol. vi. p. 301 :—

'That done, we toucht our *Beagles*, and so made
Both hills and vallies eccho to his death.'

Read, *bugles*.

Fortune by Land and Sea, vol. vi. p. 392 :—

'Come ... thy melancholy makes our teems to vaile heir foretop s, and all our Jades crestfaln, and to see thee wail in woe in the deep *cart-roots* up to the bellies plunge in pain.'

Read, *cart-ruts*.

Fortune by Land and Sea, vol. vi. p. 409 :—

'Sirrah I have a Proclamation to publish and because myself am somewhat hoarse, and thou hast a large wide mouth and *a laudible* voice,' etc.

Read, *an audible*.

Fortune by Land and Sea, vol. vi. p. 421 :—

'If please your worship here is a *manner*, or a kind of *some foul desire* to have some conference with you.'

Read, *mariner*, and *seafowl desires*, *i.e.* who desires. Old Harding asks, 'A sea-fowl?' and the Clown answers, 'Yes, a sea-gul, I mean a Mariner.'

MIDDLETON[1]

Blurt, Master Constable, I. 2. 153 :—

'*No*, sir, you are ingrost: you must give my officer a groat; it's nothing to me.'

Read, '*So*, sir,' etc.

The Phœnix, iii. 1. 60 :—

'I ha' seen the day I could have *told* money out of other men's purses.'

Qy. *toll'd*? though of course *told* may mean 'counted out.'

Michaelmas Term, ii. 3. 383 :—

'*Easy.* How like you my Roman hand, i' faith?
'*Dust.* Exceeding well, sir, but that you rest too much upon your *R*, and make your ease too little.'

Read, *R's*, for the sake of the coarse pun on *ease* and *e's*.

Mayor of Queenborough, iv. 2. 135 :—

'Her uncle and myself,
Wild *in* this tempest, as e'er robb'd man's peace,
Will undertake, upon life's deprivation,
He shall accept this oath.'

Dyce suggests, '*In this wild* tempest.' I would read, 'Wild *tho*' this tempest.'

---

[1] The references are to Bullen's edition, 8 vols. 1885-6.

The Old Law, i. 1. 207 :—

'Forty of 'em I know my seniors,
That did *due* deeds of darkness too : their country
Has watch'd 'em a good turn for't.'

Qy. ' That did *do* deeds,' etc. ?

The Old Law, i. 1. 223 :—

'I have felt nature's winters, sicknesses,
Yet ever kept a lively sap in me
To greet the cheerful spring of health again.'

Bullen would prefer 'winter-sicknesses'; but surely 'sicknesses' is in apposition with 'winters.'

The Old Law, i. 1. 320-324 :—

'Improvident, at least partial nature !
(Weak woman in this kind), who, in thy last
Teeming, forgets the former, ever making
The burden of thy last throes still the dearest
Darling ; oh yet,' etc.

This is Bullen's reading. The old edition gives :—

'Teeming *still* forgets the former, ever making
The burthen of thy last throws the dearest
Darling ; oh yet,' etc.

Gifford and Dyce give :—

'(Weak woman in this kind), who, in thy last teeming
Forgetest still the former, ever making
The burthen of thy last throes the dearest darling.'

I cannot believe that *last* was repeated as in

Dyce, Gifford, and Bullen's editions, or that *still* can have crept in. I would therefore suggest :—

> 'Who, in thy teeming
> Still *dost* forget the former, ever making
> The burthen of thy *latest* throes the dearest
> Darling; oh yet,' etc.

The Old Law, i. 1. 426 :—

> 'I cannot (this knowing) fear
> *That*, when I am gone hence, I shall be there.'

'Gifford,' Bullen notes, ' says : " The conclusion of this speech I do not understand." Should we read "here," and understand by the passage, " I cannot doubt but that, after my death, my name will live among my countrymen." Cf. l. 174, 'Buried my name in Epire."'

I would read, ' *What*, when,' etc.

The Old Law, ii. 1. 183 :—

> 'Now I would have men know what I resemble
> A truth indeed.'

Read, *A*' truth indeed, *i.e.* in truth.

The Old Law, v. 1. 148 :—

> 'More reverence to the place than to the persons:
> To the one I offer up a [spreading] palm
> Of duty and obedience [a]s to heaven,
> Imploring justice, which was never wanting
> Upon that bench whilst their own fathers sat;
> But unto you, my hands contracted thus,' etc.

Gifford remarks : 'I have inserted *spreading*,

not merely on account of its completing the verse, but because it contrasts well with *contracted*. Whatever the author's word was, it was shuffled out of its place at the press, and appears as a misprint (*showdu*) in the succeeding line.'

Perhaps under *showdu* the word concealed was *shadowing*.

The Old Law, v. 1. 225, 226 :—

'This were the judgment-seat we [stand at] now!
[Of] the heaviest crimes that euer made up [sin]
Unnaturalness and inhumanity,
You are found foul and guiltly,' etc.

This is Gifford's text for that of the old edition :—

'This were the judgment seat, we now
The heaviest crimes that ever made up,
Unnaturalness in humanity.'

'This were,' he explains as 'O, that this were.' I suggest :—

'*Were this* the judgment-seat, we now *to judge*
The heaviest crimes that ever made up *all*
Unnaturalness and inhumanity,' etc.

A Trick to catch the Old One, v. 2. 127 :—

'*Hoard.* Daintily abus'd! you've put a *junt* upon me!
Luc. Ha, ha, ha!
Hoard. A common strumpet!'

I would read 'a *punk*.'

The Family of Love, i. 2. 161 :—

'Thou wilt tomorrow, thou sayest, begone; if thou wilt know the worst of a *country's* marry before thou goest; for if thou canst endure a curst wife, never care what company thou comest in.'

Qy. Insert *curses* after *country's*?

The Family of Love, v. 2. 25 :—

> 'Aurora, now the blushing sun's approach
> Dart not more comfort to this universe
> Than thou to me.'

'Dyce,' says Bullen, ' reads :—

> "Aurora, *now* the blushing *sun approaches*";

adding, 'I suspect that the whole line is corrupted, and that the epithet "blushing" belongs to "Aurora."' The old edition gives *now*; and with Bullen's emendation *nor*, no change seems to be needed; but it would be easy to read,

> 'Blushing Aurora, nor the sun's approach.'

Your Five Gallants, ii. 1. 123 :—

> 'It is no *affliction*, gentlemen.'

Dyce suggests, 'It is *not a fiction*.' Qy. 'It is no *affection*,' *i.e.* affectation? Compare *Hamlet*, ii. 2. 464; *Love's Labour's Lost*, v. 1. 4.

Your Five Gallants, ii. 3. 337 :—

> 'Why, what's the business? *filch it on hob* goblet!'

I would read, '*filching on* (*i.e.* of) *yon* goblet!'

the blunder being possibly due to some confusion with the word 'hob-goblin.'

Your Five Gallants, iii. 5. 62 :—

'*Pur.* No less than three at once, sir,
Made a triangle with their swords and daggers,
And all opposing me.
Fit. And amongst those three only one hurt you, sir?
Pur. Ex for ex.'

Dyce queries, 'Can this expression mean "*ecce*, for example"?' I believe it is nothing more than a contraction of the old legal phrase 'except before excepted,' *exceptis excipiendis*, which in *Twelfth Night*, i. 3. 7, Sir Toby burlesques in the words, 'Why, let her *except, before excepted.*'

Your Five Gallants, iv. 7. 112 :—

'You unlucky, *maple-faced* rascal.'

Dyce remarks, 'Whether this epithet is to be explained rough-faced, or brown-faced, or broad-faced, seems doubtful. See Gifford's note on B. Jonson's Works, vol. vi. p. 156.' Gifford there suspects that the term rather refers to colour, and means tann'd, or sun-burnt, than alludes, as Malone thinks, to the rough bark of the maple. Surely the word means 'mottled,' like the grain of maple.

A Mad World, my Masters, ii. 2. 19 :—

'Tomorrow your lordship shall see my cocks, my fish-ponds, my park, my champion grounds: I keep *champers* in my house, can show your lordship some pleasure.'

Dyce suggests that *champers* perhaps means *horses*; Halliwell, *hounds*; Nares, *caters*. Surely we should read *chambers*; it is the *house* that now is being shown, and horses are not kept in houses. What *caters*, as in Bullen's copy of Nares and my own, or *eaters*, as in Dyce's, may mean, I cannot guess.

A Fair Quarrel, iii. 1. 146:—

'Sir, either draw
And that not slightingly, but with the care
Of your best preservation, with that watchfulness
As you'd defend yourself from circular fire,
Your sin's rage, or her lord—this will require it—
Or you'll be too soon lost, for I've an anger
Has gathered mighty strength against you, mighty :
Yet you shall find it honest to the last,
Noble and fair.'

I suppose Dyce and Bullen discover some sense in the italicised words, but to me they yield none whatever. It seems plain that it is a material danger of which Captain Ager speaks, and I would read, '*The sea's* rage *in* her *flood*'; supposing Y^e to have been taken for Y^r, as is so frequently the case: the two most terrible of material forces will thus have been named.

No Wit, No Help like a Woman's, ii. 3. 258:—

'What deeps I see beneath me, in whose falls
Many a nimble mortal toils
And scarce can *feed* himself.'

Conjectural Readings 175

Dyce records a friend's conjecture *fleet*, *i.e.* float, which Bullen rightly rejects. I would read *fend*.

A Chaste Maid in Cheapside, i. 1. 27 :—

'Errors? nay, the city cannot hold you, wife,
But you must needs fetch words from Westminster:
Tha' done, i' faith.'

Read, *Ha'* done, etc.

Anything for a Quiet Life, i. 1. 88 :—

'Good Sir Francis, you have had sore eyes too, you have been a gamester, but you have given it o'er; and to redeem the vice belonged to 't, you now entertain certain *farcels* of silenced ministers, which, I think, will equally undo you.'

Of *farcels* Dyce remarks that it 'is, perhaps, a word formed from the verb to *farce* (to stuff), though I have not elsewhere met with it.' Even if there were such a word, I cannot see what appositeness it would have here. I would read *parcels*, comparing *The Merchant of Venice*, i. 2. 119, 'I am glad this *parcel* of wooers are so reasonable'; *All's Well*, ii. 3. 58, 'this youthful *parcel* Of noble bachelors stand at my bestowing.'

The Witch, ii. 2. 136 :—

'By the sweet health of youth, I will be careful,
And never prate on 't, nor like a cunning snarer,
Make thy *clipp'd* name the bird to call in others.'

Bullen notes, 'Cleped, called.' But surely the metaphor is from the clipped wing of a bird in a snare, her 'clipped name' being her injured reputation. Compare below, iv. 2. 52-53:—

> 'So 'tis our trade to set snares for other women,
> 'Cause we were once caught ourselves.'

The Changeling, v. 2. 60:—

After this line, a line, to be given to Tomaso, has dropped out in Bullen's edition.

The Spanish Gipsy, ii. 1. 240:—

> 'You *told* I was some copper coin.'

Dyce queries *trowed*? Possibly the meaning is, 'You counted me for some copper coin.'

The Spanish Gipsy, iv. 1. 70:—

> 'Vow, as these flowers themselves entwine,
> Of April's wealth building a throne
> *Round, so* your love to one or none.'

Bullen suggests that we should place a comma after 'throne,' and read, '*To bound* your love,' etc. I should prefer, placing the comma after 'throne,' to read '*Bound* so your love,' etc., as an elliptical expression for 'that so your love is bound,' etc.

Women Beware Women, i. 2. 56:—

> '*Liv.* Then I must tell you
> Your money was soon parted.
> *Guar. Light her now*, brother.
> *Liv.* Where is my niece?'

Conjectural Readings

Bullen remarks, 'The text is corrupt. I fear the following emendation is hardly satisfactory:—

> "*Liv.* Then I must tell you
> Your money was soon parted.
> *Fab.* Like enow.
> *Liv.* Brother, where's my niece?"

The reader will remember that the last syllable of *enow* was frequently sounded like the adverb *now*. Between *light her now* and *like enow* there is no great difference of pronunciation.'

Assigning the speeches as in the text, I would read:—

> "'*Slight*, her *own* brother!' [*aside.*

Guardiano being surprised at Livia's sarcastic answer to Fabricio.

Women Beware Women, iii. 2. 101:—

> 'Who was't told us lately
> Of a match-making *right*, a marriage-tender?'

Qy. *rite?* The two words are often confounded.

Women Beware Women, iii. 2. 149:—

> 'What harder chance can fall to woman,
> Who was born to cleave to some man,
> Than to bestow her time, youth, beauty,
> Life's observance, honour, duty,
> On a thing for no use good,
> But to make physic work, or blood
> Force fresh in an old lady's cheek?
> She that would be
> Mother of fools, let her compound with me.'

Has a line fallen out after *cheek*? The rest of the lines rhyme regularly.

More Dissemblers Beside Women, ii. 1. 57:—

'Your goodness simple, without *gain* or art.'

Dyce queries *guile*? Possibly *fain*, *i.e.* feign.

The World Tost at Tennis, l. 300:—

'*Jup.* Were not these precedents for all future ages?
Scho. But none attains their glories, king of stars;
These are the fames are follow'd and pursu'd
But never overtaken.
Jup. The *fate's* below,
The god's arms are not shorten'd, nor do we shine
With fainter influence.'

Bullen notes, 'Qy. "The Fates bestow?" (*i.e.* the Fates are as bountiful as in former days).'

This seems to me very unsatisfactory. I would read, 'The *fault's* below,' *i.e.* it is not the impotence of the gods in bestowing, but the lack of deserving on the part of men. Compare above l. 251:—

'How can it be but they have both abus'd,
And would, *for their ills, make our justice guilty?*'

The Black Book, vol. viii. p. 14:—

'Thus in a pair of hoary slippers, his stockings dangling about his *wrists*,' etc.

I do not remember to have elsewhere met with *wrists* = ankles.

Micro-Cynicon, His Defiance to Envy, l. 6 :—

> 'Avaunt, I say ! I 'll anger thee enough,
> And fold thy fiery eyes in thy *smazky* snuff.'

Dyce says, '*i.e.* perhaps smitchy or smeechy (reechy, black).' Qy. only a misprint of *smoaky*, *i.e.* smoky?

GREENE[1]

Orlando Furioso, p. 90/1 :—

> 'And I, my lord, am Mandricard of Mexico,
> Whose climate's fairer than Iberia's,
> Seated beyond the sea of Tripoly,
> And richer than the plot Hesperides,
> Or that same isle wherein Ulysses' love
> Lull'd in her lap the young Telegonus :
> *That did but Venus tread a dainty step,*
> So would she like the land of Mexico,
> As Paphos and brave Cyprus set aside,
> With me sweet lovely Venus would abide.'

Of the line in italics Dyce remarks, 'This line—before which something has certainly dropt out—appears to be corrupted.' I doubt there being any corruption, and take the meaning to be that if Venus would only condescend to leave her usual haunts and pay a visit to Mexico, she would prefer it to Paphos, etc.

Orlando Furioso, p. 90/2 :—

> 'Swift fame hath sounded to our western seas
> The matchless beauty of Angelica,
> Fairer than was the nymph of Mercury,

---

[1] The references are to Dyce's Edition, 1 vol., 1874.

> Who when bright Phœbus mounteth up his coach,
> And tracts Aurora in her silver steps,
> *And sprinkles* from the folding of her lap
> White lilies, roses, and sweet violets.'

Dyce notes, ' In *England's Parnassus*, 1600, p. 415, this passage is quoted with the variation "*And sprinkling*," etc. I have no doubt that a line which immediately preceded the present one has dropped out. A critic in *The Retrospective Review*, iii. 111, silently prints "Doth sprinkle."'

I would read *Besprinkles*; *and* being caught from the line above, and the nymph being Maia.

Orlando Furioso, p. 92, 2 :—

> ' Honour,—methinks the title is too base ;
> Mighty, *glorious*, and excellent,—ay, these,
> My glorious genius sound within my mouth.'

Of 'glorious,' in the third line, Dyce says, ' A wrong epithet,—repeated from the preceding line.' I am inclined to think that the corruption is in the second line, and that for *glorious* we should there read *renowned*. The rhythm of the line would be improved.

Orlando Furioso, p. 95/1 :—

> ' Brave country, know, where sacred love unites,
> The knot of *gordian* at the shrine of Jove
> Was never half so hard or intricate
> As be the bands which lovely Venus ties.

> Sweet is my love; and, for I love, my lord,
> Seek not *unless*, as Alexander did,
> To cut the plough-swain's traces with thy sword,
> Or slice the slender fillets of my life:
> *Or* else, my lord, Orlando must be mine.'

For *gordian* I would read *Gordium*. On p. 96/2 Greene writes correctly 'This *gordian* knot,' and here he would scarcely use such a phrase as 'knot of *gordian*.' For *Or* Dyce would read 'For,' remarking, 'But the whole speech is corrupted.' I doubt this, and would read and punctuate thus:—

> 'Seek not, *useless*, as Alexander did,
> To cut the plough-swain's traces with thy sword:
> Or slice the slender fillets of my life,
> Or else, my lord, Orlando must be mine.'

From his punctuation, with a comma only after 'sword,' and a colon after 'life,' Dyce apparently takes the construction to be, 'To cut . . . sword, or to slice,' etc. To me it seems that the meaning is, 'Do not uselessly hope to cut the knot of the difficulty as Alexander cut the Gordian knot with his sword: *either* kill me, *or* Orlando must be mine.'

Looking-Glass for London and England, p. 142/1:—

> 'Thine eldest sister is *Lamana*,
> And Sodom on thy right hand seated is.'

Of *Lamana* Dyce says, 'Some corruption here.' The lines are a portion of Jonas's warning to

Nineveh, and the sense is that that city is own sister, and (morally) next neighbour, to the 'cities of the plain.' One of these cities was Admah, or Adama, mentioned with Sodom and Gomorrah in *Genesis*, x. 19, xiv. 2, 8; *Deuteronomy*, xxix. 23; and I would here suggest *El Adama* for *Lamana*, thereby making the line metrical.

Looking-Glass for London and England, p. 143/2 :—

'The covetous man *sorry* for his sin.'

The 4to gives '*forie* sorry'; read, '*sore* sorry.'

James the Fourth, p. 187/1 :—

'Stage direction. Music playing within, enter Aster Oberon, King of the Fairies; and Antics, who dance about a tomb placed conveniently on the stage; out of which suddenly starts up, as they dance, Bohan, a Scot, attired like a *ridstall* man.'

Of *ridstall* Dyce remarks, 'A mis-spelling, if not a corruption.' Can the word be *byr-stall*, *i.e.* cowherd?

James the Fourth, p. 192/1 :—

'. . . and if your queen repine,
Although my nature cannot brook of blood,
And scholars grieve to hear of murderous deeds,
But if the lamb should let the lion's way,
By my advice the lamb should lose her life.'

I would read *Yet*.

James the Fourth, p. 193/1 :—

'If any gentleman ... will entertain ... a young stripling ... that can sleep with the soundest, eat with the hungriest, *work with the sickest*, lie with the loudest, face with the proudest,' etc.

On *sickest* Dyce notes, ' A friend conjectures "sickerest." Qy. "stoutest?"'

Against both conjectures I object that Ateukin's catalogue of pretended qualifications is a catalogue of *dis*qualifications; and I would therefore read '*shirk* work with the sickest'; the omission of *shirk* before *work* from the similarity of sound would be very likely.

James the Fourth, p. 195/2 :—

'Go shroud us in our harbour, where we'll see
The *pride* of folly, as it ought to be.'

Dyce notes ' Qy. "prize" (*i.e.* reward)?'

I think *pride* is sound, taking 'as it ought to be' to mean 'properly represented,' not, as Dyce apparently understands, 'well-deserved.'

James the Fourth, p. 195/2 :—

'Whoso thou be that passest [by],
For I know one shall pass, know I
Am Cyrus of Persia, and I pray
Leave me not thus like a clod of clay
Wherewith my body is covered.'

'The 4to,' says Dyce, 'gives

> " I am Cirus of Persia
> And I *prithee* leave me not thus," etc.

But all this is stark nonsense. See the inscription on the tomb of Cyrus in Plutarch, *Alex.* 69.'

The inscription is as follows: 'O man, whosoever thou art, and whensoever thou comest (for come I know thou wilt), I am Cyrus, the founder of the Persian empire; *envy me not the little earth that covers my body.*' Surely, following this, we should read:—

> '*Envy* me not *this little* clod of clay.'

James the Fourth, p. 196/1:—

> 'I can no more; my patience will *not* warp
> To see these flatterers how they scorn and carp.'

Read, *but*.

James the Fourth, p. 206/2:—

> 'What, shall I jet in breeches like a squire?
> Alas, poor dwarf, *thy mistress is unmeet*!'

'Corrupted,' says Dyce; 'this line ought to rhyme with the preceding one.'

This is clear; and I would read, '*unmeet is such attire.*'

James the Fourth, p. 219/1:—

> 'Stay, princes, wage not war: a privy grudge
> 'Twixt such as you, most high in majesty,
> Afflicts both nocent and the innocent.

> How many swords, dear princes, see I drawn!
> The friend against his friend, a deadly *fiend;*
> A desperate division in those lands
> Which, if they join in one, command the world.'

The 4to gives *friend*, which Dyce alters to *fiend*. The next words, however, 'A desperate division,' show clearly that we should read *feud*. For an apparent misprint of *fiend* for *feud*, see note on p. 197.

Alphonsus, p. 225/1 :—

> 'The time hath been when Homer's sugar'd Muse
> Did make each echo to repeat his verse,
> That every coward that durst crack a spear,
> And tilt and tournay for his lady's sake,
> Was painted out in colours of such price
> As might become the proudest potentate.
> But nowadays *so irksome* idless' sleights,
> And cursed charms have witch'd each student's mind,
> That death it is to any of them all,
> If that their hands to penning you do call.'

Can *so irksome* be right? I think we should read *frolicsome*.

Alphonsus, p. 230/1 :—

> 'Pardon, Alphonsus, this my first offence,
> And let me die if e'er I *flight* again.'

Read, *slight*. It is his 'uncourteous words' for which Lælius is apologising.

George-A-Greene, p. 268/2 :—

'To mend thy living take thou Middleham-castle,
The hold of both; and if thou want *living*, complain,
Thou shalt have more to maintain thy estate.'

I would read *That*, Y^t having been mistaken for Y^e, *i.e.* hold that from both of us, King James and myself; and would omit *living*, as being caught from the line above.

DEKKER[1]

The Gentle Craft, vol. i. p. 28 :—

'They gingle in my pocket like S. Mary *Queries* bels.'

Read, *Overy's* ; a correction made in the margin of my copy. St. Mary Overy, now St. Saviour's, Southwark, was once a church of great beauty; famous, among other things, as being the burial place of Massinger, Fletcher, and Gower. It has a peal of twelve bells, nine of which are over four hundred years old. See Hare, *Walks in London*, i. 495.

The Gentle Craft, vol. i. p. 48 :—

'Say that I
Do constantly believe *you*, constant *haue*.'

Qy. 'Do constantly believe *your* constant love'?

Olde Fortunatus, Prol. l. 3. vol. i. p. 85 :—

'Of Loues sweete war, our timerous Muse doth sing,
And to the bosome of each gentle deare,
Offence her Artless tunes.'

Read, '*Offers* her artless tunes.'

---

[1] The references are to Pearson's Reprint, 4 vols. 1873.

Olde Fortunatus, vol. i. p. 91 :—

> ' Onely for sport, to see the Apish world
> Worship such beast with *sound* idolatrie.'

Read, *fond*.

Olde Fortunatus, vol. i. p. 106 :—

> ' In mockerie blowes *from his* rotten browes.'

Read, ' from *off* his.'

Olde Fortunatus, vol. i. p. 116 :—

' *Andel.* But hast no sharper reasons than this ?
' *Shad.* Yes one : the dagger in Cyprus had never stab'd out such sixe penie *pipes* but for hunger.
' *Andel.* Why, you dolt, these pies are but in their minority.'

Read, *pies*. The Dagger, in Holborn, was an ordinary famous for its pies, which were called ' dagger-pies.'

Olde Fortunatus, vol. i. p. 122 :—

> ' It had been so, if *riches* had been mine.'

Read, *wisdom*. He had chosen *riches*, and hence his ruin.

Olde Fortunatus, vol. i. p. 133 :—

> ' Till *uow*, I did *not* dally with loues fire.'

Read, *now* and *but*.

Olde Fortunatus, vol. i. p. 140 :—

> ' Here was no Princesse but *my* princely self.'

Read, *thy*.

Satiro-mastix, vol. i. p. 196 :—

'Who's there? *stray*, treade softly.'

Read, *stay*.

Satiro-mastix, vol. i. p. 204 :—

'For I ha some things that were fetcht (I am sure) as *faire* as some of the Low Countries.'

Read, *far*.

Satiro-mastix, vol. i. p. 213 :—

'The Muses birdes the Bees were hiu'd and *fled* Vs in our cradle.'

Read, *fed*.

Satiro-mastix, vol. i. p. 221 :—

'Wut thou be proude little Lucifer? well, thou shalt goe how then thou wilt Maide-marian; come busse thy little Anthony now, my cleane Cleopatria; so, so, goe thy waies *Alexis secrets*, th' a breath as sweet as the Rose, that growes by the Beare-garden, as sweete as the proud'st head a Garlicke in England.'

Of *Alexis secrets* I can make no sense, but take it to be a corruption of *alexiterick*, *i.e.* having the power to ward off infection. The allusion in the next lines is, as Collier points out, to the effluvia from the Hope bear-garden which penetrated to the Rose tavern; and Tucca vies with Pistol in his variety of names and epithets.

Satiro-mastix, vol. i. p. 229 :—

'Wher's the *sering* thou carriest about thee? O have I found thee my scowring-sticke; what's my name Bubo?'

I suppose *sering* is another spelling of *syringe*, formerly spelt *siringe*, from O. F. *seringue*, and the allusion to Horace's ink-horn from which he squirted gall upon his enemies.

Satiro-mastix, vol. i. p. 229 :—

'Death of Hercules, he could never play that part well in's life, no *Fulkes* you could not.'

I think we should read, 'no *hulks*, you could not.' The allusions to Horace's (*i.e.* Ben Jonson's) bulky stature are frequent.

The Honest Whore, vol. ii. p. 31 :—

' Belike then shee's some *sale* curtizan.'

Read, *stale*.

The Honest Whore, vol. ii. p. 33 :—

'At your best pleasure *whewsome* rubbers there.'

Read,

' At your best pleasure ; *whew ! some* rubbers there ! '

i.e. Holla, let some rubbers attend !

The Honest Whore, vol. ii. p. 44 :—

' I faith they ha pepperd me, sister : look, *dost* not spin ?'

Read, *does't i.e.* does it (*sc.* the blood) not spin from my head ? For 'spin,' of blood, cf. *H.V.* iv. 2. 10, ' That their hot blood may *spin* in English eyes.' Misprints of this trivial kind abound in this edition ; but, except where they are at all likely to obscure the sense, I do not notice them.

The Honest Whore, vol. ii. p. 52 :—

'And all you gallants can bestow on them,
Is that French Infant, which ne'er *acts*, but *speaks*.'

Transpose *acts* and *speaks*; the 'infant' of course being the *Morbus Gallicus*.

The Honest Whore, vol. ii. p. 67 :—

'A *sister's* threed yfaith had been enough
To lead me anywhere.'

Read, *spinster's*.

The Honest Whore, vol. ii. p. 69 :—

'*Itch* lurch if you will.'

Read, '*I'th* lurch,' etc.

The Honest Whore, vol. ii. p. 117 :—

'*Mat.* And an old knave, there's more deceit in him then in sixteene Poticaries : its a Deuill, thou maist beg, starue, hang, damne ; does he send thee so much as a cheese ?
'*Orl.* Or so much as a Gammon of Bacon,
He'll giue it his Dogs first.
'*Mat.* A *Jayle*, a *Jayle*.
'*Orl.* A Jew, a Jew, sir.
'*Mat.* A Dog.
'*Orl.* An English Mastiffe, sir.
'*Mat.* Pox rot out his old stinking garbage.'

For *Jayle* should we read *Javel* (*i.e.* worthless fellow)? The word, in the sense of villain, rogue, etc., occurs twice in More's *Utopia*, and twice in *Rede me and be nott wrothe*, 1528.

The Honest Whore, vol. ii. p. 156 :—
> 'I commit your Grace.'

Is this a contracted (or perhaps interrupted) form of the old conclusion of dedicatory epistles, etc., 'I commit your Grace *to the tuition of God*'? Compare *Much Ado about Nothing*, i. 1. 281, 282.

The Whore of Babylon, vol. ii. p. 219 :—
> 'They have but 17 daughters young and faire,
> Vowd to liue uestalls, *and* to know the touch
> Of any forced or vnreuerend hand.'

Read, *not*.

The Whore of Babylon, vol. ii. p. 220 :—
> 'Stands my beard right? *the* gowne I must look graue.'

Read and punctuate,
> 'Stands my beard right? *my* gown? I must,' etc.

The Whore of Babylon, vol. ii. p. 224 :—
> 'O *Yee's* unkind, hard-hearted.'

Read, *she's*.

The Whore of Babylon, vol. ii. p. 234 :—
> 'Some *lyne* sea cards, that know not the seas tast.'

Read, *limn*, *i.e.* paint.

The Whore of Babylon, vol. ii. p. 258 :—
> 'These totald vp,
> You shall a hundred thousand swordes behold
> Brandisht at once, whose——standes
> Men will seeme borne with weapons in their handes.'

N

Perhaps we may insert,

> 'Brandished at once, whose *fury who* withstands?'

If This be not a Good Play, etc. vol. iii. p. 267 :—

> 'Get thee gon :
> *That* call'd for.'

Read, *Thou'rt*.

If This be not a Good Play, etc., vol. iii. p. 305 :—

> 'Onely to *eate* a liquorish appetite
> Digst our religious *wales* up.'

Read, *sate* and *walls*.

Match Me in London, vol. iv. p. 161 :—

> 'Heare me, thou shin'st with thunder, yet this hand
> That can shake kingdomes downe, thrusts into thine
> The scepters, if proud *fall*, thou lets them fall
> Thou beat'st thyself in peeces on a rocke.'

Read, 'if proud *fool*, thou,' etc.

Match Me in London, vol. iv. p. 187 :—

> 'Why is this rose *deui'd* with a pearled teare.'

Read, *dew'd*.

The Wonder of a Kingdome, vol. iv. p. 234 :—

> 'A benefit given by a Niggards hand
> Is stale and *gravily* bread, the hunger-sterv'd
> Takes it, but cannot eate it.'

Read, *gravelly*, *i.e.* like gravel.

Conjectural Readings

The Sun's Darling, vol. iv. p. 338 :—

'Never till now
  Did admiration beget in me truly
  The rare match'd twins at once, pittie and pleasure ;
  So royal, so aboundant in earth's blessings,
  Should not partake the comfort of those beames.'

Qy. Should we insert after 'pleasure,'

  'Pleasure at this brave sight, pity that one'?

WEBSTER[1]

The White Devil, p. 23/1 :—

> 'My lord Cardinal,
> Were your intelligencing ears as loving
> *As* to my thoughts, had you an honest tongue,
> I would not care though you proclaim'd them all.'

I believe we should read and punctuate thus:

> 'Were your intelligencing ears as loving,
> *And* to my thoughts had you an honest tongue,' etc.

i.e. were your ears as ready to put a generous construction upon any rumours to my discredit as they are eager to believe such rumours, and had you an honest tongue to speak my thoughts, etc.

The White Devil, p. 46/1 :—

> 'I have liv'd
> Riotously ill, like some that live in court,
> And sometimes when my face was full of smiles,
> Have felt *the maze* of conscience in my breast.'

Surely *the maze* cannot be right: Qy. *th' amaze*?

---

[1] The references are to Dyce's edition, 1 vol. 1857.

The Devil's Law-Case, p. 127/1 :—

> 'O jealousy,
> How violent, especially in women!
> How often has it raised the devil up
> In form of a law-case! my especial care
> Must be to nourish craftily this *fiend*
> 'Tween the mother and the daughter, that the deceit
> Be not perceiv'd.'

I think we should read *feud*. It is true that Romelio speaks of raising the devil up, but he would hardly talk of nourishing 'this fiend *'tween* the mother and the daughter.' The word 'devil' would account for *fiend* instead of *feud*.

The Devil's Law-Case, p. 130/1 :—

> 'Why, you whoreson fogging rascal,
> Are these not *whores* enough for presentations
> Of overseers wrong the will o' the dead,
> Oppressions of widows or young orphans,
> Wicked divorces, or your vicious cause
> Of *Plus quam satis* to content a woman
> But you must find new stratagems, new pursenets.'

Can *whores* be right, or has it been caught from *whoreson* in the line above, and should we read *courts*? Why should whores bring cases against overseers, guardians, who mal-administer wills? What have they to do with oppressions of widows or young orphans, with wicked divorces, etc.?

The Devil's Law-Case, p. 130/2 :—

> 'Bad suits, and not the law, *bred* the law's shame.'

Qy. *breed*?

The Devil's Law-Case, p. 131/2 :—

> 'Into the noble ancient family
> Of the *Palavafini*.'

Qy. *Paravicini*?

Appius and Virginia, p. 168/2 :—

'I am amongst curs a trindle-tail, and amongst fishes a poor *iper*.'

Surely *viper*. Corbulo, though a clown, does not misuse speech.

Appius and Virginia, p. 180/1 :—

> 'Judges are term'd
> The gods on earth : and such as are corrupt
> *Read* me in this my ruin ; those that succeed me
> That so offend, thus punish.'

Qy. *Heed* (*i.e.* let them heed)?

Sir Thomas Wyatt, p. 186/2 :—

> 'Honour and happy reign.
> Attend the *new majesty* of England !'

Qy. 'new-*made* majesty'?

Sir Thomas Wyatt, p. 187/1 :—

> 'Pardon me, madam, that so boldly *I* press
> Into your chamber.'

Qy. omit *I*?

Sir Thomas Wyatt, p. 187/1 :—

'Ask that of Suffolk's duke, and great Northumberland,
Who in your stead have crown'd *another*.'

Qy. 'another *queen*'?

Conjectural Readings

Sir Thomas Wyatt, p. 187/2 :—

'Honourable friends, and native peers,
That have chosen me to be the leader
Of these martial troops, to march against,' etc.

Qy.

'*My* honourable friends, and native peers
That have *now* chosen me to be the leader
Of these *your* martial troops, to march against,' etc. ?

Sir Thomas Wyatt, p. 187/2 :—

'In your hands we leaue the queen elected :
She hath seizure of the Tower.'

Qy.

'In your *strong* hands we leave the Queen elected :
She hath *the* seizure of the Tower' ?

Sir Thomas Wyatt, p. 189/1 :—

'The obligation wherein we all stood bound
To the deceas'd *late* King's will and our decree,
His cousin Jane and the two absent dukes,
Cannot be *conceal'd* without great reproach
To us and to our issue.'

Omit *late*, and read *cancell'd*.

Sir Thomas Wyatt, p. 189/2 :—

'Besides this sacred proof, the princely maids,
Had they no will nor act to prove their right,
Have *birthrights no* privilege, being a plea so strong
As cannot be refell'd but by plain wrong.'

I would punctuate and read as follows :—

> ' Besides this sacred proof, the princely maids,—
> Had they no will nor act to prove their right,—
> Have *birthright's* privilege, being a plea so strong
> As cannot be refell'd but by plain wrong.'

Sir Thomas Wyatt, p. 192/1 :—

> 'But I am overtook, and you are kind,
> I am, beshrew *you* else.'

Read, *me*.

Sir Thomas Wyatt, p. 193/1 :—

> 'This is the place where I betray'd my lord ;
> This is the place where oft I have *reliev'd*,
> And villain, I betray'd him to the jaws of death.'

Read, *retir'd*.

Sir Thomas Wyatt, p. 195/2 :—

> ' *Guild.* The nights are tedious, and the days are sad :
> And see you how the people stand in heaps,
> Each man sad-looking on his oppos'd object,
> As if a general passion possessed them ?
> Their eyes do seem as dropping as the moon,
> As if prepared for a tragedy ;
> For never swarms of people there do tread,
> But to rob life and to enrich the dead,
> And *show* they wept.
> *Lieut.* My lord, they did so, for I was there.'

On the last line but one of the passage Dyce remarks, ' Either something which preceded these words has dropt out, or else they are corrupted.'

I would enclose the lines ' For never . . . dead '

in brackets as being parenthetical, and read *sure* for *show*. The Lieutenant's answer clearly indicates this change.

Sir Thomas Wyatt, p. 196/2 :—

'No knave, Sir Thomas ; I am a true man
To *my queen*, to whom thou art a traitor.'

Qy. 'To my *dear* queen'?

Sir Thomas Wyatt, p. 203/2 :—

'A ruddy lip, a clear reflecting eye,
Cheeks purer than the maiden orient pearl,
That sprinkle bashfulness *through* the clouds.'

'Corrupted, of course,' says Dyce, '(the old copies have "That sprinkle*s*," etc.).' I think the old copies are right, and that with *thorough* for *through* the passage is sound. The idea is similar to that in *Orlando Furioso*, p. 90/2 :—

'Who when bright Phœbus mounteth up his coach,
And tracts Aurora *in her silver steps*' :

the 'bashfulness' being the ruddy glow that causes Aurora to blush as her silver steps advance.

Westward Ho, p. 216/1 :—

'I think, when all's done, I must follow his counsel, and take a patch ; I['d] have had one long ere this, but for disfiguring my face : yet I had noted that a mastic patch upon some women's temples hath been the very *rheum* of beauty.'

Of *rheum*, Dyce says, 'A misprint, I believe; but qy. for what?' I think undoubtedly for *crown*.

Westward Ho, p. 217/1 :—

'It's the fault of many that fight under this *band*.'

Qy. *banner?*

Northward Ho, p. 263/1 :—

'Come, my little punk, with thy two compositors to the unlawful *painting*-house, thy *pounders*: my old poetical dad will be here presently.'

The old edition has 'thy pounders *a* my old poeticall dad,' etc. Dyce says, 'I am doubtful about the right reading.'

I think we should certainly read, 'Come . . . to this unlawful *printing*-house; thy *type*-founders *and* my old,' etc. There is, of course, an indelicate equivoque in 'compositors,' 'printing-house,' and 'type-founders.'

Northward Ho, p. 267/2 :—

'A thousand pound to a penny she spoil *not* her face, or break her neck, or catch a cold that she may ne'er claw off again.'

Qy. omit *not*? Though in such constructions old writers were often very weak in their logic.

Northward Ho, p. 280/1 :—

'Why, look you, *was he* aware of those *broken patience* when you met him at Ware and possessed him of the downfall of his wife.'

For *patience* Dyce suggests *patients*; I know not with what meaning. I would read:—

'Why, look you, *I was* aware of those *broking pretences* when you met him . . . wife.'

Bellamont was present throughout the meeting at Ware between Mayberry on the one side and Greenshield and Featherstone on the other, when the latter gentlemen relate how they won Mrs. Mayberry's love.

INDEX I

Of passages discussed

BEAUMONT AND FLETCHER:—

				PAGE
Beggar's Bush,	iii. 4 vol.	ix.	p. 67,	75
,, ,,	v. 2 ,,	,,	p 103,	75
Bloody Brother, The,	iii. 1 ,,	x.	p. 413,	85
,, ,,	iv. 1 ,,	,,	p. 431,	86
Bonduca,	i. 1 ,,	v.	p. 7,	62
Coxcomb, The,	ii. 2 ,,	iii.	p. 152	47
,, ,,	ii. 3 ,,	,,	p. 157,	47
,, ,,	iv. 2 ,,	,,	p. 181,	49
Cupid's Revenge,	i. 1 ,,	ii.	p. 363,	41
,, ,,	ii. 2 ,,	,,	p. 378,	41
,, ,,	ii. 6 ,,	,,	p. 393,	41
,, ,,	v. 4 ,,	,,	p. 441,	41
Double Marriage, The,	v. 3 ,,	vi.	p. 409,	67
Elder Brother, The,	iii. 1 ,,	x.	p. 235,	80
,, ,,	iii. 3 ,,	,,	p. 242,	81
,, ,,	v. 1 ,,	,,	p. 286,	82
,, ,,	v. 2 ,,	,,	p. 289,	83
Fair Maid of the Inn, The,	ii. 2 ,,	x.	p. 36,	77
,, ,, ,,	iii. 1 ,,	,,	p. 49,	77
,, ,, ,,	iii. 2 ,,	,,	p. 53,	77
,, ,, ,,	iii. 2 ,,	,,	p. 53,	77
Faithful Friends, The,	i. 1 ,,	iv.	p. 200,	60
,, ,,	i. 1 ,,	,,	p. 204,	61
,, ,,	iv. 1 ,,	,,	p. 273,	61
Faithful Shepherdess, The,	i. 1 ,,	ii.	p. 26,	36
,, ,,	ii. 2 ,,	,,	p. 48,	37
,, ,,	ii. 3 ,,	,,	p. 55,	39
,, ,,	iii. 1 ,,	,,	p. 64,	40
False One, The,	ii. 2 ,,	vi.	p. 250,	66
,, ,,	iv. 3 ,,	,,	p. 289,	67

			PAGE
Four Plays in One; The Triumph of Honour.	Sc. i. vol. ii. p. 490,		42
,, ,, ,,	Sc. ii. ,, ,, p. 499,		45
Four Plays in One; The Triumph of Death.	Sc. iv. ,, ii. p. 552,		46
,, ,, ,,	Sc. v. ,, ,, p. 554,	.	47
Honest Man's Fortune, The,	i. 1 ,, ii. p. 345,	.	40
Humorous Lieutenant, The,	iii. 5 ,, vi. p. 478,	.	68
Island Princess The,	iii. 1 ,, vii. p. 458,	.	70
Knight of Malta, The,	ii. 2 ,, v. p. 134,	.	62
,, ,,	iii. 4 ,, ,, p. 167,	.	63
,, ,,	iv. 2 ,, ,, p. 186,	.	63
Laws of Candy, The,	iii. 3 ,, v. p. 364,	.	64
Love's Pilgrimage,	iii. 2 ,, xi. p. 277,	.	87
Loyal Subject, The,	iv. 3 ,, vi. p. 85,	.	65
,, ,,	iv. 4 ,, ,, p. 88,	.	65
Mad Lover, The,	Epil. l. 2 vi. p. 212,	.	66
Maid's Tragedy, The,	i. 2 ,, i. p. 338,	.	34
,, ,,	ii. 2 ,, ,, p. 359,	.	36
Monsieur Thomas,	ii. 3 ,, vii. p. 338,	.	70
,, ,,	iii. 1 ,, ,, p. 349,	.	70
Nice Valour, The,	ii. 1 ,, x. p. 305,	.	83
,, ,,	ii. 1 ,, ,, p. 314,	.	84
,, ,,	v. 1 ,, ,, p. 358,	.	84
Night Walker, The,	iii. 6 ,, xi. p. 175,	.	86
Noble Gentleman, The,	i. 2 ,, x. p. 123,	.	78
,, ,,	iii. 2 ,, ,, p. 149,	.	78
,, ,,	v. 1 ,, ,, p. 187,	.	79
Philaster,	i. 1 ,, i. p. 218,	.	33
Pilgrim, The,	ii. 2 ,, viii. p. 30,	.	71
Queen of Corinth,	i. 2 ,, v. p. 404,	.	65
,, ,,	iii. 1 ,, ,, p. 440,	.	65
Rule a Wife, etc.,	i. 2 ,, ix. p. 403,	.	76
Scornful Lady, The,	ii. 3 ,, iii. p. 44,	.	47
Sea-Voyage, The,	i. 2 ,, viii. p. 302,	.	73
Spanish Curate, The,	v. 2 ,, ,, p. 481,	.	74
Thierry and Theodoret,	i. 1 ,, i. p. 109,	.	31
,, ,,	i. 1 ,, ,, p. 111,	.	31
,, ,,	i. 1 ,, ,, p. 111,	.	31
,, ,,	iii. 1 ,, ,, p. 149,	.	32
,, ,,	v. 1 ,, ,, p. 189,	.	33

			PAGE
Two Noble Kinsmen, The,	i. 4	vol. xi. p. 351,	88
Valentinian,	iv. 4	,, v. p. 287,	64
Widow, The,	i. 2	,, iv. p. 318,	61
,, ,,	v. 1	,, ,, p. 381,	62
Wife for a Month, A,	i. 4	,, ix. p. 326,	76
Wild-Goose Chase, The,	i. 1	,, viii. p. 117,	72
,, ,,	iv. 1	,, ,, p. 176,	72
Wit at Several Weapons,	i. 2	,, iv. p. 16,	49
Wit without Money,	i. 1	,, iv. p. 111,	50
,, ,,	ii. 2	,, ,, p. 119,	52
,, ,,	ii. 2	,, ,, p. 121,	53
,, ,,	iii. 1	,, ,, p. 139,	54
,, ,,	iii. 1	,, ,, p. 139,	54
,, ,,	iii. 1	,, ,, p. 142,	55
,, ,,	iv. 2	,, ,, p. 159,	55
,, ,,	iv. 4	,, ,, p. 172,	56
,, ,,	iv. 5	,, ,, p. 176,	56
,, ,,	v. 2	,, ,, p. 184,	60
Woman's Prize, The,	ii. 4	,, vii. p. 139,	68
,, ,,	ii. 4	,, ,, p. 140,	69
,, ,,	ii. 6	,, ,, p. 144,	69
Women Pleased,	iv. 1	,, ,, p. 57,	68

CHAPMAN:—

All Fooles,	vol. i. p. 143,	128
,,	,, ,, p. 150,	128
,,	,, ,, p. 168,	128
Alphonsus,	,, iii. p. 218,	143
Blind Beggar of Alexandria, The,	,, ii. p. 5,	127
,, ,,	,, ,, p. 24,	127
,, ,,	,, ,, p. 29,	127
Bussy d'Ambois,	,, ii. p. 10,	131
,,	,, ,, p. 59,	131
,,	,, ,, p. 82,	132
Byrons Conspiracie,	,, ,, p. 186,	133
,,	,, ,, p. 211,	134
,,	,, ,, p. 223,	134
,,	,, ,, p. 241,	135
,,	,, ,, p. 254,	135
,,	,, ,, p. 255,	135

		PAGE
Byrons Tragedie,	vol. ii. p. 256,	135
,,	,, ,, p. 282,	135
,,	,, ,, p. 285,	136
,,	,, ,, p. 288,	136
,,	,, ,, p. 292,	136
,,	,, ,, p. 296,	136
,,	,, ,, p. 304,	136
,,	,, ,, p. 306,	136
,,	,, ,, p. 307,	136
,,	,, ,, p. 312,	137
,,	,, ,, p. 314,	137
,,	,, ,, p. 318,	138
Cæsar and Pompey,	,, iii. p. 136,	141
,,	,, ,, p. 152,	142
,,	,, ,, p. 155,	142
,,	,, ,, p. 167,	142
,,	,, ,, p. 168,	142
,,	,, ,, p. 171,	143
,,	,, ,, p. 174,	143
Gentleman Usher, The,	,, i. p. 258,	130
,, ,,	,, ,, p. 267,	130
,, ,,	,, ,, p. 268,	130
,, ,,	,, ,, p. 283,	130
,, ,,	,, ,, p. 315,	131
,, ,,	,, ,, p. 538,	131
Humerous Dayes Mirth,	,, ,, p. 54,	128
,, ,,	,, ,, p. 58,	128
May-Day,	,, ii. p. 335,	138
,,	,, ,, p. 347,	138
,,	,, ,, p. 366,	138
,,	,, ,, p. 371,	138
,,	,, ,, p. 376,	138
,,	,, ,, p. 379,	139
,,	,, ,, p. 384,	139
,,	,, ,, p. 385,	139
,,	,, ,, p. 386,	139
Monsieur d'Olive,	,, i. p. 211,	128
,,	,, ,, p. 212,	129
,,	,, ,, p. 220,	129
,,	,, ,, p. 235,	130
Revenge of Bussy d'Ambois, The,	,, ii. p. 108,	132

Index I

		PAGE
Revenge of Bussy d'Ambois, The,	vol. ii. p. 113,	133
,, ,,	,, ,, p. 134,	133
,, ,,	,, ,, p. 143,	133
Revenge for Honour,	,, iii. p. 290,	143
,,	,, ,, p. 293,	143
,,	,, ,, p. 301,	144
,,	,, ,, p. 317,	144
Widdowes Teares, The,	,, iii. p. 48,	139
,, ,,	,, ,, p. 55,	140
,, ,,	,, ,, p. 69,	140
,, ,,	,, ,, p. 70,	140
,, ,,	,, ,, p. 71,	140
,, ,,	,, ,, p. 82,	141

DEKKER:—

Gentle Craft, The,	vol. i. p. 28,	188
,, ,,	,, ,, p. 48,	188
Honest Whore, The,	,, ii. p. 31,	191
,, ,,	,, ,, p. 33,	191
,, ,,	,, ,, p. 44,	191
,, ,,	,, ii. p. 52,	192
,, ,,	,, ,, p. 67,	192
,, ,,	,, ,, p. 69,	192
,, ,,	,, ,, p. 117,	192
,, ,,	,, ,, p. 156,	193
If this be not a good Play, etc.,	,, iii. p. 267,	194
,, ,, ,,	,, ,, p. 305,	194
Match me in London,	,, iv. p. 161,	194
,, ,,	,, ,, p 187,	194
Olde Fortunatus,	,, i. p. 85,	188
,, ,,	,, ,, p. 91,	189
,, ,,	,, ,, p. 106,	189
,, ,,	,, ,, p. 116,	189
,, ,,	,, ,, p. 122,	189
,, ,,	,, ,, p. 133,	189
,, ,,	,, ,, p. 140,	189
Satiro-Mastix,	,, i. p. 196,	190
,, ,,	,, ,, p. 204,	190
,, ,,	,, ,, p. 213,	190
,, ,,	,, ,, p. 221,	190
,, ,,	,, ,, p. 229,	190

		PAGE
Sun's Darling, The,	vol. iv. p. 338,	195
Whore of Babylon, The,	,, ii. p. 156,	193
,, ,,	,, ,, p. 219,	193
,, ,,	,, ,, p. 220,	193
,, ,,	,, ,, p. 224,	193
,, ,,	,, ,, p. 234,	193
,, ,,	,, ,, p. 258,	193
Wonder of a Kingdom, The,	,, iv. p. 234,	194

GREENE :—

Alphonsus,	p. 225/1,	186
,,	p. 230/1,	187
George-a-Greene,	p. 268/2,	187
James the Fourth,	p. 187/1,	183
,,	p. 192/1,	183
,,	p. 193/1,	184
,,	p. 195/2,	184
,,	p. 195/2,	184
,,	p. 196/1,	185
,,	p. 206/2,	185
,,	p. 219/1,	186
Looking-Glass for London, A, etc.,	p. 142/1,	182
,, ,, ,,	p. 143/2,	183
,, ,, ,,	p. 187/1,	183
Orlando Furioso,	p. 90/1,	180
,,	p. 90/2,	180
,,	p. 92/2,	181
,,	p. 95/1,	181

HEYWOOD :—

Age, Brazen, The,	vol. iii. p. 174,	153
,, ,,	,, ,, p. 196,	154
,, ,,	,, ,, p. 235,	154
,, ,,	,, ,, p. 249,	154
Age, Golden, The,	iii. ,, p. 26,	152
,, ,,	,, ,, p. 40,	152
,, ,,	,, ,, p. 68,	153
,, ,,	,, ,, p. 69,	153
I. Age, Iron, The,	,, iii. p. 273,	154
,,	,, ,, p. 288,	154

Index I

		PAGE
I. Age, Iron, The,	vol. iii. p. 304,	154
,,	,, ,, p. 309,	154
,,	,, ,, p. 313,	155
,,	,, ,, p. 331,	155
,,	,, ,, p. 333,	155
,,	,, ,, p. 337,	155
,,	,, ,, p. 339,	155
,,	,, ,, p. 345,	156
II. Age, Iron, The,	,, ,, p. 368,	156
,,	,, ,, p. 370,	156
,,	,, ,, p. 406,	156
,,	,, ,, p. 409,	157
,,	,, ,, p. 420,	157
Age, Silver, The,	iii. ,, p. 91,	153
,,	,, ,, p. 100,	153
,,	,, ,, p. 159,	153
Challenge for Beauty, A,	,, v. p. 9,	161
,, ,,	,, ,, p. 12,	161
,, ,,	,, ,, p. 13,	161
,, ,,	,, ,, p. 17,	162
,, ,,	,, ,, p. 23,	162
,, ,,	,, ,, p. 39,	162
,, ,,	,, ,, p. 47,	162
,, ,,	,, ,, p. 48,	162
,, ,,	,, ,, p. 59,	163
,, ,,	,, ,, p. 73,	163
,, ,,	,, ,, p. 77,	163
Earth and Age,	,, vi. p. 134,	165
,,	,, ,, p. 138,	165
I. Edward the Fourth,	,, i. p. 83,	145
,, ,,	,, ,, p. 105,	145
II. Edward the Fourth,	,, ,, p. 119,	145
,, ,,	,, ,, p. 156,	146
,, ,,	,, ,, p. 160,	146
,, ,,	,, ,, p. 166,	147
English Traveller, The,	,, iv. p. 16,	157
,, ,,	,, ,, p. 22,	157
,, ,,	,, ,, p. 26,	157
,, ,,	,, ,, p. 73,	158
,, ,,	,, ,, p. 87,	158

			PAGE
Faire Maide of the Exchange, The,	vol. ii. p. 40,	.	148
,, ,,	,, ,, p. 47,	.	149
,, ,,	,, ,, p. 64,	.	149
,, ,,	,, ,, p. 69,	.	149
,, ,,	,, ,, p. 78,	.	150
Faire Maide of the West, The, .	,, ii. p. 287,	.	152
,, ,,	,, ,, p. 384,	.	152
,, ,,	,, ,, p. 389,	.	152
Fortune by Land and Sea,	,, vi. p. 392,	.	166
,, ,,	,, ,, p. 409,	.	166
,, ,,	,, ,, p. 421,	.	167
Foure Prentises of London, The,	,, ii. p. 219.	.	151
,, ,,	,, ,, p. 251,	.	151
If you know not Me, etc.,	,, i. p. 197,	.	147
,, ,,	,, ,, p. 239,	.	147
,, ,,	,, ,, p. 245,	.	147
,, ,,	,, ,, p. 270,	.	147
,, ,,	,, ,, p. 307,	.	148
Jupiter and Io, .	,, vi. p. 273,	.	166
Loues Mistris, .	,, v. p. 98,	.	163
,, ,,	,, ,, p. 136,	.	164
,, ,,	,, ,, p. 137,	.	164
Man-Hater, The,	,, vi. p. 158,	.	165
,, ,,	,, ,, p. 191,	.	166
Mayden-head well Lost, A,	,, iv. p. 110,	.	158
,, ,,	,, ,, p. 127,	.	158
,, ,,	,, ,, p. 128,	.	158
,, ,,	,, ,, p. 130,	.	159
,, ,,	,, ,, p. 146,	.	159
,, ,,	,, ,, p. 156,	.	159
,, ,,	,, ,, p. 164,	.	159
Pelopæa and Alope, .	,, vi. p. 301,	.	166
Procus and Puella, .	,, ,, p. 122,	.	165
Rape of Lucrece, The,	,, v. p. 246,	.	164
Wise-woman of Hogsdon, The,	,, ,, p. 281,	.	164
,, ,,	,, ,, p. 319,	.	164
,, ,,	,, ,, p. 330,	.	164
,, ,,	,, ,, p. 333,	.	164
Witches of Lancashire, The,	,, iv. p. 178,	.	159
,, ,,	,, ,, p. 181,	.	159

			PAGE
Witches of Lancashire, The,	vol. iv.	p. 182,	159
,, ,,	,, ,,	p. 189,	160
,, ,,	,, ,,	p. 191,	160
,, ,,	,, ,,	p. 196,	160
,, ,,	,, ,,	p. 199,	160
,, ,,	,, ,,	p. 207,	160
Woman Kild with Kindnes,	,, ii.	p. 99,	150
,, ,,	,, ,,	p. 111,	151
,, ,,	,, ,,	p. 115,	151
,, ,,	,, ,,	p. 121,	151

MARLOWE:—

Dido,	iii. 2.	3,	122
,,	iv. 1.	4,	122
,,	iv. 5.	28,	123
,,	v. 1.	110,	123
,,	v. 1.	221,	123
,,	v. 1.	276,	124
Faustus, Chorus,	l. 2.		119
Hero and Leander, First Sestiad,	l. 477.		125
Jew of Malta, The,	i. 1.	4,	120
,, ,,	i. 2.	283,	120
,, ,,	ii. 1.	44,	121
,, ,,	iv. 1.	124,	121
,, ,,	iv. 4.	74,	122
Ovid's Elegies,	iii. 7.	29.	125
I. Tamburlaine,	v. 1.	117,	116
,,	v. 1.	183-187,	116
,,	v. 1.	236,	117
II. Tamburlaine,	i. 3.	147,	118
,,	iii. 2.	99,	118
,,	v. 3,	188,	119
,,	v. 3,	199,	119

MARSTON:—

I. Antonio and Mellida,	i. 1.	258,	1
,, ,,	ii. 1.	14,	1
,, ,,	iii. 2.	99,	2
,, ,,	iii. 2.	107,	2
,, ,,	iii. 2.	125,	2

			PAGE
I. Antonio and Mellida,	iv. 1. 70,		3
,, ,,	iv. 1. 80,		3
II. Antonio and Mellida,	i. 1. 73,		4
,, ,,	i. 1. 76,		4
,, ,,	i. 2. 130-132,		4
,, ,,	ii. 1. 58,		5
,, ,,	ii. 1. 154,		5
Dutch Courtezan, The,	ii. 2. 214, 215,		7
,, ,,	iii. 1. 17,		7
,, ,,	v. 2. 139,		7
Eastward Ho,	iv. 1. 43,		20
Fawn, The,	ii. 1. 101,		8
,,	ii. 1. 179,		8
,,	ii. 1. 197,		8
,,	ii. 1. 218,		8
,,	ii. 1. 151,		8
,,	iii. 1. 214,		9
,,	iii. 1. 254,		9
,,	iii. 1. 354,		9
,,	iv. 1. 133,		9
,,	iv. 1. 397,		10
,,	v. 1. 213,		10
,,	v. 1. 406,		11
Insatiate Countess, The,	i. 1. 97,		20
,, ,,	i. 1. 108,		21
,, ,,	ii. 2. 28-34,		21
,, ,,	iii. 2. 7,		22
,, ,,	iii. 2. 46,		23
,, ,,	iii. 4. 52,		23
,, ,,	iii. 4. 96,		23
,, ,,	iv. 2. 66,		24
,, ,,	iv. 5. 17,		25
,, ,,	iv. 5. 22,		25
,, ,,	v. 1. 4,		26
,, ,,	v. 1. 42,		26
Malcontent, The,	iv. 2. 112,		5
,, ,,	v. 1. 9,		6
,, ,,	v. 2. 262,		6
,, ,,	v. 2. 286,		6
,, ,,	v. 3. 154,		7
Scourge of Villainy, The,	i. 2. 135,		27

Index I

				PAGE
Scourge of Villainy, The,	.	iii. 11. 33,	. .	29
,, ,,	.	iii. 11. 54.	. .	29
Sophonisba,	. . .	i. 2. 12,	. .	11
,,	. . . .	i. 2. 76,	. .	11
,,	. . . .	i. 2. 83,	. .	12
,,	. . . .	i. 2. 169,	. .	12
,,	. . . .	i. 2. 228,	. .	13
,,	. . . .	ii. 2. 71,	. .	13
,,	. . . .	iii. 1. 63,	. .	13
,,	. . . .	iii. 1. 147,	. .	14
,,	. . . .	iii. 2. 7-9,	. .	14
,,	. . . .	iii. 2. 73,	. .	14
,,	. . . .	v. 3. 36, 37,	. .	15
,,	. . . .	v. 1. 89,	. .	15
What You Will,	. .	Ind. l. 106,	. .	15
,,	. . .	,, 111,	. .	15
,,	. . .	Prol. 15,	. .	15
,,	. . .	i. 1. 102,	. .	16
,,	. . .	i. 1. 119,	. .	16
What You Will,	. .	ii. 1. 51,	. .	16
,, ,,	. .	ii. 1. 149,	. .	16
,, ,,	. .	ii. 2. 45,	. .	16
,, ,,	. .	ii. 2. 90,	. .	17
,, ,,	. .	ii. 2. 134,	. .	17
,, ,,	. .	ii. 2. 106,	. .	17
,, ,,	. .	iii. 2. 16,	. .	18
,, ,,	. .	iii. 2. 93,	. .	18
,, ,,	. .	iii. 2. 117,	. .	18
,, ,,	. .	iv. 1. 96, 97,	. .	18
,, ,,	. . -	iv. 1. 127,	. .	19
,, ,,	. .	iv. 1. 140-146,	. .	19
,, ,,	. .	iv. 1. 181, 182,	. .	20
,, ,,	. .	iv. 1. 238, 241,	. .	20

MIDDLETON :—

Anything for a Quiet Life, .	i. 1. 88, . .	. 175
Blurt, Master Constable, .	i. 2. 153, . .	. 168
Chaste Maid in Cheapside, A, .	i. 1. 27, . .	. 175
Fair Quarrel, A, . .	iii. 1. 146, . .	. 174
Family of Love, The, .	i. 2. 161, . .	. 172
,, ,, . .	v. 2. 25, . .	. 172

			PAGE
Mad World, my Masters, A,	ii. 2. 19,		173
Mayor of Queenborough,	iv. 2, 135,		168
Michaelmas Term,	ii. 3. 383,		168
Micro-Cynicon,	l. 6,		179
More Dissemblers Beside Women,	ii. 1. 57,		178
No Wit, No Help, etc.,	ii. 3. 258,		174
Old Law, The,	i. 1. 207,		169
,,	i. 1. 223,		169
,,	i. 1. 320-324,		169
,,	i. 1. 426,		170
,,	ii. 1. 183,		170
,,	v. 1. 148,		170
,,	v. 1. 225, 226,		171
Phœnix, The,	iii. 1. 60,		168
Spanish Gipsy, The,	ii. 1. 240,		176
,, ,,	iv. 1. 70,		170
Trick to catch the Old One, A,	v. 2. 127,		171
Witch, The,	ii. 2. 136,		175
Women Beware Women,	i. 2. 56,		176
,, ,,	iii. 2. 101,		177
,, ,,	iii. 2. 149,		177
World Tost at Tennis, The,	l. 300,		178
Your Five Gallants,	ii. 1. 123,		172
,, ,,	ii. 3. 337,		172
,, ,,	iii. 5. 62,		173
,, ,,	iv. 7. 112,		173

PEELE:—

Arraignment of Paris, The,	i. 1. 84,		89
,, ,,	iii. 1. 121,		89
Battle of Alcazar, The,	i. 2. 1,		103
,, ,,	i. 2. 38, 39,		104
,, ,,	i. 2. 54,		105
,, ,,	ii. 4. 19,		105
,, ,,	ii. 4. 120, 121,		105
,, ,,	v. 1. 9-11,		108
,, ,,	v. 1. 37,		109
,, ,,	v. 1. 252,		109
David and Bethsabe,	sc. i. 67,		109
,, ,,	,, i. 85,		109
,, ,,	,, i. 106, 115,		110

Index I

				PAGE
David and Bethsabe,	sc.	iii. 95,	.	111
,, ,,	,,	iii. 137,	.	112
,, ,,	,,	v. 26,	.	112
,, ,,	,,	viii. 106,	.	113
,, ,,	,,	xi. 13,	.	113
Edward I.,	.	iii. 39-41,	.	90
,,	,,	iii. 81,	.	91
,,	,,	iii. 93,	.	92
,,	,,	iii. 95,	.	93
,,	,,	iii. 107-114,	.	93
,,	,,	vii. 91, 92,	.	94
,,	,,	x. 85-90,	.	96
,,	,,	xi. 1-8,	.	96
,,	,,	xviii. 8,	.	98
,,	,,	xxv. 9,	.	98
,,	,,	xii. 155,	.	100
,,	,,	xxv. 18,	.	100
,,	,,	xxv. 29,	.	101
,,	,,	xxv. 70,	.	101
,,	,,	xxv. 113,	.	101
,,	,,	xxv. 118, 120,	.	102
,,	,,	xxv. 182,	.	102
,,	,,	xxv. 269,	.	103
Praise of Chastity, The,	.	l. 43.	.	114
Sir Clyomon and Sir Clamydes,	sc. xi. 96,	.	114

WEBSTER:—

Appius and Virginia,	p. 168/2,	198
,, ,,	p. 180/1,	198
Devil's Law-case, The,	p. 127/1,	197
,, ,,	p. 130/1,	197
,, ,,	p. 130/2,	197
,, ,,	p. 131/2,	198
Northward Ho,	p. 263/1,	202
,, ,,	p. 267/2,	202
,, ,,	p. 280/1,	202
Westward Ho,	p. 216/1,	201
,, ,,	p. 217/1,	202
White Devil, The,	p. 23/1,	169
,, ,,	p. 46/1,	169
Wyatt, Sir Thomas,	p. 186/2,	198

218 Conjectural Readings

		PAGE
Wyatt, Sir Thomas,	p. 187/1,	198
,, ,,	p. 187/2,	199
,, ,,	p. 189/1,	199
,, ,,	p. 189/2,	199
,, ,,	p. 192/1,	200
,, ,,	p. 193/1,	200
,, ,,	p. 195/2,	200
,, ,,	p. 196/2,	201
,, ,,	p. 203/2,	201

INDEX II

Of Principal Emendations Proposed

TEXT	EMENDATION	PAGE
Abbeys,	Rabble,	96
About,	Without,	18
About phases,	About faces,	11
Aie,	Vie,	118
Alexis secrets,	Alexiterick,	190
Amaze,	A maze,	15
And sprinkles,	Besprinkles,	181
Arch for truth,	Arch foe to truth,	147
Ay,	Joy,	7
Banishing,	Publishing,	5
Banishment,	Punishment,	128
Baus'd,	Brows'd,	17
Beans,	Beeves,	51
Bekindled,	Be kindled,	112
Belief must arrive,	He lief must arride,	132
Bloody bound	Flood y-bound,	113
Bones' fair covering,	Beams far hovering,	110
Breadth,	Brain,	130
Bring a long globe,	Being a blown globe,	137
Broken patience,	Broking pretences,	203
Cæsar's,	Ease's,	62

Index II

TEXT	EMENDATION	PAGE
Cæsar's brain,	Ceres' brow,	102
Cancel,	Counsel,	77
Canero,	Cancro,	140
Care,	Crare,	66
Carpell,	Carol,	97
Cherelly,	Cheerbelly,	77
Conceal'd,	Cancell'd,	199
Condition,	Coition,	23
Coistered,	Hoistered	6
Corb'd,	Coopèd,	5
Count,	Commit,	144
Countermined,	Countermured,	120
Damn'd,	Daub'd,	5
Daughter,	Drugster,	124
Death,	Grief,	4
Deceive,	Deserve,	144
Deem'd,	Queen'd,	25
Deui'd,	Dew'd,	194
Divine,	Darraign,	84
Earth,	Breath.	137
Earth,	Warmth,	109
Embraced,	Enforced,	20
Entering carles,	Enticing curls,	131
Expalcat	Expatiate,	143
Fair,	Fire,	110
Faith,	Fall,	73
Fame-insatiate,	Same insatiate,	21
Farcels,	Parcels,	175
Femelacy,	Simulacracy,	23
Fiend,	Feud,	186
Fiend,	Feud,	197
Filch it on hob goblet,	Filching on yon goblet,	172
Flames,	Veins,	101
Flatten,	Shotten,	68
Flight,	Slight,	187
Follow,	Fellows,	31
Fore-handed,	Free-handed,	47
Forth,	Fourth,	27
Frame,	Flame,	112
Froth,	Forth,	1
Frozen,	Proven,	98

TEXT	EMENDATION	PAGE
Fulkes,	Hulks,	191
Furcug,	Curtius-gulf,	53
Giris,	Gyges,	129
Give,	Grieve,	81
Go farewell,	Forgo farewell,	123
Gom,	Gum,	62
Haue,	Love,	188
Hunt,	Heart,	55
Imbast,	Impaste,	125
Infant,	In faint,	17
Interpret,	Penetrate,	9
I'ternally abandon,	Eternally abandon'd,	20
Jayle,	Javel,	192
Jest,	Pest,	9
Jove,	Love,	95
Lamana,	El Adama,	182
Lansket,	Wainscot,	69
Last,	Lust,	3
Last night,	Lastingest,	148
Leaders,	Peal does	157
Leave,	Envy,	185
Leaves,	Braves,	143
Leaveth,	Feareth,	6
Let the blow,	Laid them low.	155
Liege,	Siege,	102
Like,	Little,	185
Limit,	Invite,	164
London's,	Love's,	149
Looks,	Locks,	102
Lov'd of her,	Lord of Himen,	10
Lucky,	Lusty,	84
Lure,	Air,	125
Lyne,	Limn,	193
Mad,	Made,	61
Mad,	Made,	135
Man,	Wan,	21
Nellson,	Keelson,	60
Neptolis,	Niphates,	26
No hurt,	Honour,	163
Not,	Most,	40
O'er-pry the palms,	O'er-breathe your balm,	92

Index II

TEXT	EMENDATION	PAGE
Offence,	Offers,	188
Over-hied,	Over-vy'd,	72
Painting,	Printing,	202
Partly,	Pardy,	112
Party,	Parting,	79
Passing,	Paying,	161
Perceives,	Pursues,	70
Pipes,	Pies,	189
Play,	Splay,	107
Ployden,	Hoyden,	7
Reliev'd,	Retir'd,	200
Renew'd,	Enew'd,	150
Rest,	Rise,	26
Resting,	Resty,	111
Rheum,	Crown,	201
Riches,	Wisdom,	189
Ring,	Rug,	47
Robe,	Orb,	91
Ruin'd,	Rubi'd,	88
Rumnillo,	Bromhille,	51
Sale,	Stale,	191
Samintes,	Samarites,	120
San ceo,	San cielo,	29
Sayle,	Soil,	162
Scratch,	Snatch,	56
Seize,	Ease,	93
Sering,	Syringe,	191
Sest,	Pest,	18
Show.	Sure,	200
Sign,	Sinew,	146
Sins holp thee,	Foes bold them,	98
So irksome,	Frolicsome,	186
Sister,	Spinster,	192
So lawful to brave,	So, la, mi, fa, to't, raise,	97
Soul,	Scroll,	142
Sound,	Fond,	189
Steps,	Lips,	129
Strangle,	Strangling,	43
Stray,	Stay,	190
Tempest,	Topmost,	117
Tenant,	Truant,	140

TEXT	EMENDATION	PAGE
Theamea,	The Aniena,	59
The flies,	Then she flies,	95
Thou honour of ill,	Dishonour of all,	46
Thy pounders,	Thy type-founders,	202
Tire,	Tice,	149
Too fast,	To fist,	125
Too keend,	To kind,	123
Travense,	Tavern's,	2
Traitors,	Tritons,	107
Tread,	Read,	105
Tretably,	Trotably,	17
Turning,	Girning,	31
Types,	Styles,	109
Uselesse,	Cureless,	24
Vails,	Maids,	13
Wake,	Weale,	67
Wave,	Warn,	79
Weaking,	Wasting,	23
Whores,	Courts,	197
Worthy feat,	Worth thy feat,	72
Your sin's rage, or her lord,	The sea's rage in her flood,	174

THE END

www.ingramcontent.com/pod-product-compliance
Lightning Source LLC
Chambersburg PA
CBHW021837230426
43669CB00008B/1000